*Parent Partnership
Services for Special
Educational Needs*

Home and School – A working alliance

This series, edited by *John Bastiani* and *Sheila Wolfendale*, brings together wide-ranging contributions which

- are written from both professional and parental viewpoints
- offer an assessment of what has been achieved
- explore a number of problematic issues and experiences
- illustrate developments that are beginning to take shape.

It appeals to those with a special interest in and commitment to home–school work in all its actual and potential facets.

Series titles

Parent Partnership Services for Special Educational Needs

Celebrations and Challenges

Edited by
Sheila Wolfendale

David Fulton Publishers

London

David Fulton Publishers Ltd
Ormond House, 26–27 Boswell Street, London WC1N 3JZ

www.fultonpublishers.co.uk

First published in Great Britain in 2002 by David Fulton Publishers

British Library Cataloguing in Publication Data
A catalogue record for this book is available from the British Library.

ISBN 1-85346-839-8

Typeset by Keyset Composition, Colchester, Essex
Printed and bound in Great Britain by The Cromwell Press, Trowbridge, Wilts.

Contents

The contributors

Roger Bishop is the Director of SNAP Cymru. He was previously an Assistant Director of Social Services and earlier an Assistant Director with the children's charity NCH. A qualified social worker, he is a parent of four sons, one of whom has special educational needs.

Ann Braham became the Parent Partnership Coordinator in the London borough of Islington in 1999. She has 30 years' experience of working in SEN, as a teacher, trainer and manager in Inner London. This present post brings together a lifelong interest in a holistic approach to pupils with SEN and in adult and family learning.

Sheila Clarkson works as an Educational Psychologist with the Plymouth Psychology Service, from which she is currently seconded, on a part-time basis, as an Academic and Professional tutor to the MEd Educational Psychology course at Exeter University. Before local government reorganisation she was with the Devon Schools' Psychological Service in West Devon and she was the Coordinator for the original Parent Partnership scheme from 1994 to 1997.

Chris Goodwin-King began teaching in 1973. After 13 years she moved into the Nottinghamshire SEN Support Service. Hertfordshire LEA appointed her to the role of Parent Partnership Coordinator in January 1995, a role she still performs. Chris now leads a Parent Partnership team within the recently formed Children, Schools and Families.

Angela Jackman is the Parent Partnership Officer for Walsall LEA. She has been a teacher for over 30 years. Since the 1980s she has been head teacher of two schools for children whose main learning difficulty was their physical disability. She is the mother of a child with a 'hidden disability': a mental health problem which meant him missing an entire year from secondary education.

Eithne Leming worked as a teacher for 16 years in both mainstream and special schools in London and Suffolk. Prior to becoming Parent Partnership Officer in September 1994, she worked as Project Manager for Suffolk's English as an Additional Language service. Eithne is author of the book, *Working with Parents*, published by the Secondary Heads Association in November 2000.

Jill Lloyd's early career was spent in personnel management in the BBC, engineering and local government. As Essex Project Manager for Kids' Clubs Network she piloted training and other work which led to the government childcare strategy. She is a member of the County Carers Strategy Group and several multidisciplinary joint planning forums and is an adviser to her local Council for Voluntary Service. Since 1997 she has been Director of Families InFocus (Essex), a charity supporting families of children with disabilities and special needs.

Chris Onions works part-time with the Plymouth Psychology Service as an Educational Psychologist. Since 1999, he has been seconded, two days a week, to work with the Plymouth Parent Partnership Service as the LEA's Parent Partnership Support Leader. When not working for Plymouth, he works for EAS (Educational Advisory Services) as an independent educational consultant and trainer.

Roger Parnell works for the Workers' Educational Association (WEA) and is the Coordinator of the WEA Parent Partnership Service in the South West. He was appointed to his current post in 1998, following a successful National Lottery bid by the WEA to continue and extend the service throughout Devon and Cornwall.

Dave Reid is Parent Partnership Officer in Hampshire Local Education Authority. He has a BA in Business Organisation and a Diploma in Careers Guidance. He has varied experience within Cleveland, West Sussex, Surrey and Hampshire Careers Services – specialising in work with the unemployed, employers and special needs. He established the Parent Partnership Service in Hampshire in 1994.

Philippa Russell is Director of the Council for Disabled Children and a Commissioner with the Disability Rights Commission. She is an Associate Director of the National Development Team for People with Learning Disabilities and a member of the Ministerial SEN Implementation Working Group and of the National Learning Disability Task Force.

Philippa Stobbs' background is in teaching and school inspection. She joined the Council for Disabled Children in 1990. Since then she has worked on a wide range of policy and practice issues for children with special educational needs and disabilities, including the co-ordination of the Council's support for the National Parent Partnership Network. She is a member of the General Teaching Council.

Sheila Wolfendale has been a primary school teacher and remedial teacher, an educational psychologist in several LEAs and is currently Director of a Doctorate in Educational Psychology programme for practising educational psychologists at the University of East London. She is the author of many books and articles on aspects of special needs, early years, assessment and parental involvement.

She carried out (with Gill Cook) an evaluation of SEN Parent Partnership Schemes for the DfEE (1995–1997) and in 2001 she completed an evaluation (with Trevor Bryans) of SEN Parent Partnership in Wales.

Part 1

National Contexts and Developments in Parent Partnership Services

Chapter 1

An account of the genesis and growth of Parent Partnership Services

Sheila Wolfendale

Introduction

This chapter aims to describe the creation and evolution of Parent Partnership Services, contextualise the broader scene of parental involvement in special needs and in education, introduce the book and describe its purpose and contents. The narrative will include reference to a number of theoretical and ideological issues, which are expanded upon by chapter authors.

Above all else, the book sets out to describe and celebrate the advent of a provision for parents and carers of children with special needs (henceforth abbreviated to the encompassing term of 'parents') which, by a number of criteria (see below) can be deemed to be unprecedented and innovative. The original terms of reference for Parent Partnership Services from their inception in 1994, were set out within the DfEE Grants for Education and Support (GEST) programme, namely:

> to encourage partnership between parents, LEAs, schools and voluntary bodies in the work of identifying, assessing and arranging provision for pupils with SEN, particularly but not necessarily all those who are statutorily assessed and have statements of SEN. The development of active partnership schemes, including the provision of information and advisory services for parents of SEN children and the identification of 'Named Persons' is intended to reduce conflict and minimise the number of statutory SEN appeals.

The later definition of Parent Partnership Services contained in the revised SEN Code of Practice couched in terms of aims (DfES 2001b) echoes these initial terms of reference, and any points of departure reflect the evolution of such services, described in this book, as well as contemporary requirements:

> The aim of parent partnership services is to ensure parents of children with special needs, including the very young, have access to information, advice and guidance in relation to the educational needs of their children

so they can make appropriate, informed decisions. The Service should provide advice to the parents of all children with SEN not only those with statements.

(DfES 2001b, para 2.19)

Providing these definitions at the outset of the chapter serves to set the scene; the chronology of Parent Partnership Services is discussed later in the chapter.

Parent-professional relations: the broader picture

These broader dimensions, including home–school links and issues of partnership, equality, empowerment have been extensively chronicled (Bastiani and Wolfendale 1996; Hornby 2000; Leming 2000; Vincent 2000; Wolfendale and Bastiani 2000). Over the past 20–30 years, the parental presence has permeated into a number of educational areas, shown by these examples:

- numbers of parent representatives on schools' governing bodies;
- parental representation on education committees;
- the requirement since 1998 for on-entry to school Baseline Assessment schemes to report to parents the results of assessment;
- the requirement, since 1999, for schools to have and to operate home–school agreements;
- the provision, within many schools and LEAs, of family literacy and family numeracy schemes, as part of the national strategy on literacy and numeracy;
- consulting parents within Ofsted schools' inspection;
- the government 'flagship' early intervention initiative, Sure Start, targeted initially at committees and families in socio-economically depressed areas, and requiring parental involvement in devising and submitting Sure Start bids (contact Sure Start Unit[1] for further information);
- the DfEE (now DfES) promotion of the concept of parents as partners on the 'learning journey' as evinced by the publication of the DfEE booklets for parents on how to support their children's learning (DfEE 2000) and the (periodic) DfES Parents' Magazine (2001a).

Other, education-related initiatives include:

- expansion of parenting education and support programmes; see the 2001 Mapping Survey into provision in England and Wales (NFPI 2001);

---

[1]Sure Start Unit, DfES, Level 2, Caxton House, Tothill Street, London, SW1H 9NA.

- the requirement for parents to be included as members of Early Years Development and Childcare Partnerships (DfEE 2001).

So many of these initiatives have cross-links to each other intentionally built into their ideology and structure; inclusion of parents is nowadays perceived to be an integral part of inter- and multi-disciplinary provision – see Wolfendale in Wolfendale and Bastiani (2000: 7) for a 'rich picture' of many of these initiatives depicting the cross-linking, and demonstrating an overall collective commitment to partnership.

Partnership with parents in the area of special needs

In the past 20–25 years, developments in this area have run parallel to and been interwoven with some of the initiatives listed above. Specific post-Warnock Report (Warnock 1978) landmarks in the SEN area which signify extension of parental rights and involvement in special needs assessment and provision include:

- the 1981 'SEN' Education Act (which became the 1993, then the 1996 Education Act) with specified rights of parents;
- continued growth of the Portage programme, wherein parents of young children with special needs work on early learning programmes for their children in tandem with practitioners (White 1997);
- creation and growth of local, regional and national parents' groups, and groups representing parents of children with special needs, for example, Parents for Inclusion (see Paige-Smith 1997);
- advent of the 1994 SEN Code of Practice (DfEE 1994) which set out the principles of partnership with parents and proposed means by which, at successive Code Stages, these could be put in practice;
- the inclusion in 1994 into GEST funding of grants to support the introduction of SEN Parent Partnership Schemes (see Wolfendale 1997).

Current SEN legislation and the revised SEN Code of Practice in respect of parent partnership are discussed.

Concepts of partnership and empowerment

The Warnock Report (1978) in the chapter entitled 'Parents as Partners' unequivocally endorsed the notion that delivery of special needs could only be effective if parents had full access to information and support and were involved in special needs assessment and decision-making processes on equal terms as professionals. It is worth repeating a key sentence from Warnock, since it has resonated down the years and was repeated in the Code of Practice (DfEE 1994): 'Parents can be effective partners only if professionals take notice of what they say and of how they express their needs, and treat their contribution as intrinsically important' (Warnock Report 1978, para. 9.6: 151).

Because a number of surveys of the 1980s attested to parental dissatisfaction with the apparently slow realisation of partnership in practice, Parent Partnership Services were created to accelerate cooperative working practices (see their rationale on p. 1).

A linked concept to 'partnership' is that of 'empowerment' which can be viewed as the active manifestation of a partnership relationship, wherein all parties mandate each other to exercise their rights and responsibilities. Family-focused service delivery regards parents as being fully participant in service planning, delivery and evaluation (Ball 1997; Wolfendale 1999; Wolfendale and Einzig 1999).

Carpenter (2000) advocates family-focused service delivery and offers these parameters for effective collaboration:

> In order to provide effective services for our families, we must understand and respect them as roles in families differ according to situations and cultures, and may not fit stereotypic assumptions. Families themselves will provide the key to support.
>
> (2000: 137)

He goes on to ask: 'The challenge is to enable and empower families but are we ready to align professional practice with family need?' (ibid.: 142). Readers will have, through this book, an opportunity to judge the extent to which partnership and empowerment practice has been realised.

The genesis of Parent Partnership Services

The GEST element was included in three successive financial years, 1994–95, 1995–96 and 1996–97. A number of criteria were laid out against which to judge bids by local education authorities which overall stressed the need for manifest commitment by them to actively implement partnership practice in a variety of ways, within the context of the 1993 Education Act and the 1994 Code of Practice. Objectives for the three years of the scheme (which applied only to England) were set out and were reproduced on p. 1. This remit upon those LEAs with GEST grants (which supplied 60 per cent of the total money, with the LEAs providing the remaining 40 per cent) was broad and paved the way for LEA personnel to use their own initiative in how they deployed the money.

Schemes and their activities

On the whole, although there were variations between LEAs, schemes were up and running within an impressively short time in the majority of LEAs. Surveys, reports (Furze and Conrad 1997), accounts (in Wolfendale 1997) and data from the National Parent Partnership Network (NPPN) database (see Chapter 3) confirm a number of activities common to the majority of these early schemes, such as:

- the creation of a key post, usually designated as Parent Partnership Officer (PPO) employed by the LEA as lead person to implement the GEST scheme;
- the preparation and distribution of written materials for parents on local SEN provision and on statutory assessment procedures;
- the initiation of a local Named Person scheme, including provision of training opportunities and support for volunteers who wish to become Named Persons (cf. SEN Code of Practice, DfEE 1994: 128).

These were the bedrock activities of schemes; a number of other activities were also noted by the above-cited reports and surveys but which varied in their occurrence. These included:

- establishment by the PPO of links with schools, particularly SEN Coordinators (SENCOs);
- creation of parents' consultative and support groups;
- forging of working links with local/national voluntary organisations;
- systems for monitoring scheme effectiveness.

The National Parent Partnership Network (NPPN) based at the Council for Disabled Children was created (with a DfEE grant) to provide a communication, information-exchange and support forum for PPOs and their colleagues. Regular newsletters, periodic conferences, training events and the creation of a comprehensive database on Parent Partnership Services have also served to validate them (see Chapter 3 for a full account).

Evaluating the impact and effectiveness of Parent Partnership Services

Research was commissioned by the DfEE to assess the impact of the schemes. The one-year study was carried out in 1996–97 by this author and Gill Cook (Research Fellow). The research aims were as follows:

- to identify outcomes and provision of parent partnership schemes in a range of different circumstances;
- to identify the effects of the schemes upon parents of children with special educational needs as well as upon the LEA, school and other involved personnel;
- to identify factors that promote effective partnership practice;
- to make recommendations, based on these good practice indicators, as to how parent partnership schemes can be sustained.

The research was primarily a multi-method qualitative study, utilising case-study methodology. Core data collection focused on 25 case-study LEAs selected on a combination of characteristics and criteria. We visited each of these and, using a semi-structured interview schedule, interviewed the Parent Partnership Officer (Coordinator) (PPO), his/her line manager, the key SEN officer and the Principal Educational Psychologist. We explored their views on progress of their Parent Partnership Scheme (PPS), progress towards partnership and scheme future directions. Focus groups of parents in each LEA were also held. Completed questionnaires were also sent in to us by a number of Named Persons in each LEA. Additionally, PPOs were asked: (a) to provide information on referrals; (b) to describe the range of their activities and contacts; and (c) to send the researchers the documentation produced by their schemes/LEAs for parents on SEN assessment procedures and local provision.

From the research study there was strong evidential support for the view that Parent Partnership Services have made a difference. Their advent in the LEA SEN milieu and culture has been a significant addition to local SEN provision and services and has catalysed thinking about how these services can most effectively be made available to parents. Those parents who have availed themselves of the support on offer perceive the key post of PPO to be a positive source of information, support and reassurance.

Respondents generally felt that there was encouraging progress towards partnership but there is still much yet to achieve, particularly in schools and also in encouraging more parents to avail themselves of the Parent Partnership Services. The Named Persons scheme was generally successful but, it was felt, required continuing investment of time, and training and support resources to maintain it effectively within LEAs.

The full report provides further details of the research process and findings, offers a quality assurance model for Parent Partnership Services and concludes with recommendations within four main spheres of operation: the organisation and place of Parent Partnership Services; Parent Partnership Service role and activities;

relations with schools; and quality assurance and review (Wolfendale and Cook 1997).

Following this piece of research, the DfEE then commissioned the National Children's Bureau (NCB) to undertake research into identifying good practice in a number of Parent Partnership Services areas, such as: links with schools, school–parent partnership in SEN, and the involvement of voluntary sector agencies. The NCB Study (Vernon 1999) illuminated practice in these areas, and offered pointers to the continuing evolution of Parent Partnership Services.

Legitimating Parent Partnership Services

Accumulating evidence from the above-mentioned studies plus NPPN activities (see Chapter 3) indicated the significant impact that Parent Partnership Services have had upon the SEN sector within English local education authorities (in respect of Wales, see Chapter 10).

Parent Partnership Services were well established, although not universal, by the time the new Labour government issued its paper *Meeting Special Educational Needs: A Programme of Action* (DfEE 1998), which stated, 'From 1999, we will expect all LEAs to have a parent partnership scheme' (ibid.: 12, para 8). This section went on to anticipate what would eventually be contained within the revised SEN Code of Practice, and the 2001 Special Educational Needs and Disability Act (SENDA), namely:

- that the revised SEN Code of Practice would elaborate upon those requirements for LEAs to have Parent Partnership Services; would set out minimum standards for services; and would offer guidance on organising these in the form of an accompanying SEN Tool Kit.
- that SENDA would require an LEA to 'arrange for the parent of any child in their area with SEN to be provided with advice and information about matters relating to those needs' (Section 2,332 A (1).

The government plans to extend the Disability Discrimination Act (DDA) 1995 to cover every aspect of education, and new duties upon schools and LEAs will come into force in September 2002. SENDA amends the DDA and inserts requirements (Part IV) to prevent discrimination against disabled children and young people in their access to education (including further and higher education).

An accompanying Code of Practice, also to be implemented in September 2002, issued by the Disability Rights Commission, is circulating in draft form for consultation at the time of writing this chapter. It includes cross-reference to Parent Partnership Services and emphasises how vital the home–school dialogue is in these words:

> For all schools, discussions with parents and pupils themselves will be important in informing the responsible body more precisely about the nature of the adjustments that may be needed in anticipation of a particular pupil being admitted . . . to the extent that information is shared, responsible bodies will be better able to make individual adjustments that are appropriately tailored.
>
> (Disability Rights Commission 2001: 62, 420, and see Chapter 2)

It would seem, from these developments and contemporary legislation, that Parent Partnership Services have become permanent features on the educational scene. Indeed, reference to them is often included within Ofsted reports of LEA inspection, and Parent Partnership Services, as an education-based service, (mostly) are as subject to 'best value' processes as any other. Indeed, in the revised SEN Code of Practice, LEAs are expected to 'take responsibility for setting and monitoring the overall standard of the service and ensure it is subject to Best Value principles' (DfES 2001b, para 2.18).

Further evidence as to the 'coming of age' of Parent Partnership Services and of the legitimacy of Parent Partnership Coordinators as a distinct professional group comes from the formation, in 1999, of the National Association of Parent Partnership Services (napps). Chapter 4 describes the aims and activities of napps.

Parent Partnership Services – range, diversity and issues

Service personnel would agree that they offer core and related services, each varying to a greater or lesser degree. The practice illustrations in Part 2 of this book bear this out. This extract from a Parent Partnership Services Information for Parents and Carers leaflet affirms a number of core activities:

- We can listen to concerns about your child's education and discuss options for action with you.
- We can inform you of your rights and responsibilities.
- We can provide information on a range of special educational needs.
- We can find answers to questions you may have about the assessment process.
- We can put you in contact with parent support groups.
- We can give you information about other sources of voluntary or professional support and advice.

- We can accompany you to meetings, such as the Annual Review of your child's statement of special educational needs.
- We can help you to write parental advice, complete forms or draft letters to the LEA.
- We do not tell you what to do or take decisions on your behalf. Our aim is to ensure that your voice is heard and that you are actively involved in any decisions that affect your child.

(With acknowledgements to the London Borough of Sutton PPS)

The National Parent Partnership Network (NPPN), via its newsletter and members' (all Parent Partnership Services) Information Exchange has been chronicling services' activities since 1996, (for further information see Chapter 3 and contact NPPN sources). By Autumn 2001 there had been 12 such Information Exchanges, each of which has taken a specific theme and which has portrayed the range of service practice. Themes have included:

- Monitoring and Evaluation;
- Support at Transition Stage;
- Working Schools;
- Consultation with Disabled Children and Young People;
- Mediation and Conflict Resolution;
- Working with Voluntary Organisations; and
- Independent Parental Supporters.

This list of topics conveys a flavour of Parent Partnership Services' areas of work and from individual service accounts we can see local and regional variations, which are bound to reflect, to some extent, local circumstances, patterns of provision and priorities.

From NPPN and napps documentation, service accounts and evaluation reports, articles, book chapters (see Wolfendale 1997) and this book, we have an accumulating canon of contemporary practice in England (see Chapter 10 regarding the position in Wales). While this denotes a *prevalent* model of operation, it cannot be said that there is, or should be, *one* Parent Partnership Services model. Organisation, structures, and employment arrangements may be similar between services, but they are not and cannot be identical. For example, most Parent Partnership Services are part of LEA SEN (see Chapters 5, 6, 7) but many have partnership or working arrangements with one or more local/national voluntary organisations (see Chapters 8 and 9 and Chapter 10 for the unique situation in Wales).

Inevitably, when the majority of Parent Partnership Coordinators and Parent Partnership Services colleagues are employed by the LEA, issues of independence and impartiality arise, and indeed, since the inception of Parent Partnership Services this has been a central and recurring issue. A prevalent view of the parents who comprised Focus Groups in the DfEE Parent Partnership Services evaluation (Wolfendale and Cook 1997) was that they were so relieved to have an available service and access to listening, sympathetic, supportive and SEN-knowledgeable Parent Partnership Services staff that this outweighed issues of independence.

However, a counter-view is that LEA-employed Parent Partnership Services staff cannot offer truly 'independent', i.e. unbiased advice. The keyword often used by parent partnership coordinators on the whole is 'neutrality', and evidently, from the accounts of satisfied 'consumers' (parents, carers), the existence of the provision is perceived by them to be more valuable *per se* than professional issues to do with being potentially compromised and having conflicts of interest. Two significant areas of Parent Partnership Services work do illustrate the continuing contentious nature of independence and associated tensions which will be briefly explored below.

Independent Parental Supporters

The reader is reminded that the provision of 'Named Persons' was built into the original Parent Partnership Scheme model (see p. 1) and indeed the provision and training of these volunteers to offer support to parents have been a core feature of Parent Partnership Services' work. The DfEE SEN Programme of Action (DfEE 1998), already alluded to, signalled a change of name and designation from Named Person to Independent Parental Supporter (IPS) and stated 'we will expect Parent Partnership Services to ensure that the parents of any child identified as having SEN should have access to an IPS' (ibid.: 13, para. 9, and see the revised SEN Code of Practice (DfES 2001b)). Services have continued to offer IPS training and to develop local cadres of such volunteers, who may be other parents, ex/retired education professionals, or people from other backgrounds.

The NPPN has recently undertaken a national survey of IPS provision (NPPN, July 2001) and, although the response rate was slightly below 50 per cent (i.e. 67 returns out of a possible total of 162 Parent Partnership Services), the data is illuminating. Sixty-one services have overall responsibility for the arrangements of recruiting, training and supervising IPSs locally, and six have made alternative arrangements, of which several have outsourced their IPS to the voluntary sector, and two LEAs have some form of service level agreement with the voluntary sector to provide the IPS Service within their LEA (see Chapters 8 and 9).

It is worth quoting verbatim the speculations offered in the NPPN IPS Survey about outsourcing:

No specific reason was given by any of the authorities who had chosen to outsource their IPS service as to why they had taken this particular course of action. It has been suggested that they chose this route primarily to ensure that parents would view IPS services as independent and impartial of the LEA. It has also been suggested that one of the benefits of outsourcing the IPS services to voluntary sector has been to free up parent partnership coordinators to undertake more strategic and development work.

(NPPN, July 2001: 2)

A snapshot of views from a small focus group of IPS, interviewed as part of an interim evaluation of the London Borough of Sutton Parent Partnership Service (Wolfendale 2001) encapsulates the independence dilemma: they commented thus: 'How can parents get their head round the LEA link and IPS independence since ultimately the LEA controls the scene?'

Mediation, conciliation and disagreement resolution

A number of Parent Partnership Services have developed arrangements or made provision for mediating/resolving disputes between parents of children with SEN and their LEAs, and this area of work has been extensively explored by NPPN (Chapter 3). Mediation/ conciliation (now commonly referred to as disagreement resolution) was referred to in the DfEE SEN Programme of Action (DfEE 1998) in the same section (p. 13, 9) as mention of Parent Partnership Services, and the requirement was expressed thus: 'We will expect LEAs to establish conciliation arrangements, with an independent element, for resolving disputes with parents.' The DfEE commissioned Jane Hall to undertake research into these developments. The main objectives of this research (Hall 1999) were: to determine the level of current mediation approaches; to examine a range of models; to identify best practice; to highlight and disseminate lessons learned; and to make recommendations. The research identified a range of operational models, encompassing direct involvement from Parent Partnership Coordinators, working for their own or another LEA, other LEA personnel, such as educational psychologists, likewise offering a mediation service, and variations upon these models. The report (Hall 1999) offers a wealth of observations, identifies issues and makes recommendations drawn from her findings which have helped inform future directions of such services.

The 2001 SEN and Disability Act (SENDA) (as well as the revised SEN Code of Practice) set out requirements thus:

332B Resolution of disputes

(1) A local education authority must make arrangements with a view to avoiding or resolving disagreements between authorities . . . and parents . . .
(2) A local education authority must also make arrangements with a view to avoiding or resolving, in each relevant school, disagreements between the parents of a relevant child and the proprietor of the school about the special educational provision made for that child.

(2001: 4)

It goes on to explicitly state '(6) The arrangements cannot affect the entitlement of a parent to appeal to the (SEN) Tribunal' (ibid.: p. 4). Extent of Parent Partnership Services involvement with the SEN Tribunal (SENT), henceforth to be known as SENDIST, the Special Educational Needs and Disability Tribunal, to encompass disability rights (see Chapter 2) has likewise varied significantly between services.

These varying arrangements for involvement by Parent Partnership Services with disagreement resolution and the SENT have posed real issues about independence/neutrality. A way forward is with new DfES-instigated arrangements to provide grants to the 11 nationwide SEN Regional Partnerships to assist them in developing the independent element for avoiding and resolving disagreements between parents of children with SEN and the LEA, and between parents and schools. Regional pools of independent mediators/ conciliators will be created, drawing heavily upon the services and expertise of local/national voluntary agencies, and surely, too, drawing upon the extensive accumulated experience and skills of local and regional Parent Partnership Services. See Gersch and Gersch (2002, in press) for discussion of issues and models of practice.

Evolution and directions of Parent Partnership Services

The chapters in Part 2 of this book exemplify the range and diversity of Parent Partnership Services. These are evolving constantly, as the Parent Partnership Service personnel develop provision and expertise, refine their *modus operandi*, forge working links with other agencies, and respond to new SEN/disability legislation, accompanying regulations and guidance. Parent Partnership Services have matured and found a distinctive identity, and they can be regarded as an integral part of local, inclusive SEN Services. While the hope might be that all LEA/local SEN interaction with parents would be 'parent friendly', if not full partnership in the empowerment sense referred to earlier in the chapter, certainly the Parent Partnership Service needs to operate partnership practice, by definition.

In common with other education services, they have to demonstrate Best Value and need to be seen to offer an accountable, quality service. There are a number of appropriate quality assurance models (see Wolfendale and Cook 1997 for a proposed 'tailor-made' model for Parent Partnership Services), of which the Sinclair *et al.* model (1997) is one, and which offers these 'seven As' attributes of effective services: available; acceptable; affordable; accessible; accountable; appropriate; and across agency. They propose potentially five outcome perspectives: outcomes for the child; family outcomes; professional outcomes; service outcomes; and public outcomes.

There is increasing emphasis upon evidence-informed practice (NCB Highlight No. 170, 1999a) and there is every indication to suppose that Parent Partnership Services are evolving accountable, evidence-based mechanisms to demonstrate their impact and effectiveness.

One area of still-evolving work, alluded to in various chapters of this book, is Parent Partnership Service engagement with schools. The aforementioned DfEE-commissioned evaluation studies identified this area as being undeveloped, partly by virtue of insufficient opportunity and inadequate Parent Partnership Service staffing levels and partly by schools not being sufficiently knowledgeable about or being proactive with their local Parent Partnership Service.

The revised SEN Code of Practice sets out at the end of Chapter 2, a list of roles and responsibilities upon LEAs, schools, the voluntary sector and Parent Partnership Services. Envisaged roles and responsibilities of schools in relation to forging and sustaining effective dialogue/partnership with parents include schools actively seeking to develop active partnerships with local parent support groups and voluntary organisations and, of course, their local Parent Partnership Service.

There is much work to do for schools and Parent Partnership Services to evolve and maintain effective working relationships. A recent survey (Rathbone/Centre for Inclusive Education and SEN, spring 2001) confirms that:

- schools often do not seek out or use parental information about their children;
- many parents continue to feel excluded from involvement with schools about their children's progress, difficulties, reviews;
- many parents are not aware of the existence or purpose of Parent Partnership Services;

- many schools fail to inform parents of local services for them, such as the Parent Partnership Services.

Recommendations from this survey of 36 LEAs includes 'the role of Parent Partnerships needs greater clarification'. As it is incumbent upon school SENCOs to foster parent partnership, they and local Parent Partnership Services need to evolve imaginative ways of effecting this. One method could be to develop skills and method-ologies in holding and running school-based family conferences (NCB Highlight No. 169, 1999b; Seligman 2000, also mentioned in Hall 1999: 14 and 53). These could bridge gaps and have the potential to explore and resolve issues at an early stage as well as offering a multi-disciplinary forum for direct dialogue with parents.

It is to be hoped that this necessarily brief overview of recent and contemporary Parent Partnership Service practice will set the scene for the chapters that follow.

Criteria for inclusion of chapters in the book

The first chapter of an edited book usually gives a brief introduction to the chapters and their authors. As editor, I also wish to state, for the record, that this book illustrates, in a selective way, the tremendous amount of good, innovative Parent Partnership Service practice. It cannot do full justice to all the Parent Partnership Services in exis-tence; it can only present a sample of contemporary practice. The authors themselves present their own and others' work.

We hope that readers will forgive omissions of a much wider spread of services and will understand that the criteria for choice include Parent Partnership Services that combine typical (to all services) with distinctive features. These criteria were adopted in approaching authors for Part 2 (practice illustrations):

- that the LEA Parent Partnership Services described are well established;
- that a geographical range is represented;
- that chapters presenting parent-led perspectives are included;
- that partnership between the LEA and voluntary organisations is described;
- that all services described offer a range of provision;
- that some chapters also provide an account of developed specialism or distinctive features.

Each author was asked to describe the genesis and evolution of their service, to highlight issues, and discuss future directions of parent partnership work in their localities. The resulting collection portrays a 'rich picture' of the range and diversity of contemporary practice, highlights the unique ways in which each service has developed, exemplifies how individual services have liaised and forged working relationships with other local services and provides indicators as to likely future service directions. The future status of Parent Partnership Services is that, from 2002, they become statutory and therefore, as opposed to recent uncertainties, their future seems guaranteed. Longer-term planning is facilitated by their new secure status.

I would like to thank each chapter author for their contributions, for being so willing to share their experiences, and for cooperating with my editorial demands.

References

Ball, M. (1997) *Consulting with Parents*. London: Early Years Network.

Bastiani, J. and Wolfendale, S. (eds) (1996) *Home-School Work in Britain: Review, Reflection and Development*. London: David Fulton Publishers.

Carpenter, B. (2000) 'Sustaining the family: meeting the needs of families of children with disabilities', *British Journal of Special Education*, **27**(3), September, 135–44.

DfEE (1994) *Code of Practice on the Identification and Assessment of Special Educational Needs*. London: DfEE.

DfEE (1994–7) *Grants for Education and Support*. London: DfEE.

DfEE (1998) *Meeting Special Educational Needs: A Programme of Action*. London: DfEE.

DfEE (2000) *Learning Journey: Guides for Parents*: Vol. 1. 3–7 years, Vol. 2. 7–11 years, Vol. 3. 11–16 years. London: DfEE.

DfEE (2001) *Early Years Development and Childcare Partnerships, Planning Guidance 2001–2002*. London: DfEE.

DfES (2001a) *Parents and Schools*. Parents' magazine. London: DfES.

DfES(2001b) *(Revised) Special Educational Needs Code of Practice*. London: DfES.

Disability Rights Commission (DRC) (2001) *The Disability Discrimination Act 1995 (as amended by the SEN and Disability Act 2001) – Consultation on a New Code of Practice (Schools)*. Available from DRC Helpline 08457 622 633.

Furze, T. and Conrad, A. (1997) 'A review of parent partnership schemes'. Chapter 7 in Wolfendale, S. (ed.) *Working with Parents of SEN Children after the Code of Practice*. London: David Fulton Publishers.

Gersch, I. and Gersch, A. (eds) (2002, in press) *Resolving Disputes in Special Education: A Practical Guide to Conciliation*. London: Routledge.

Hall, J. (1999) *Resolving Disputes Between Parents, Schools and LEAs: Some Examples of Best Practice*. London: DfEE.

Highlight No. 170 (1999a) *Evidence-based Child Care Practice*. London: National Children's Bureau.

Highlight No. 169 (1999b) *Family Group Conferences*. London: National Children's Bureau.

Hornby, G. (2000) *Improving Parental Involvement*. London: Cassell Education.

Leming, E. (2000) *Working with Parents*. Leicester: Secondary Heads Association Publications.

National Family and Parenting Institute (NFPI) (2001) *National Mapping of Family Services, in England and Wales: A Consultation Document*. London: NFPI.

National Parent Partnership Network (NPPN) (2001) *Independent Parental Supporters*. Information Exchange 12, July. London: NPPN.

Paige-Smith, A. (1997) 'The rise and impact of the parental lobby: including voluntary groups and the education of children with learning difficulties or disabilities', Chapter 4 in Wolfendale, S. (ed.) *Working with Parents of SEN Children after the Code of Practice*. London: David Fulton Publishers.

Rathbone Special Education Advice (2001, Spring) *An Analysis of How Well Mainstream Schools Involve the Parents of Pupils with SEN*. Manchester: Rathbone.

Seligman, M. (2000) *Conducting Effective Conferences with Parents of Children with Disabilities*. London: The Guilford Press.

Sinclair, R., Hearn, B. and Pugh, G. (1997) *Preventive Work with Families: The Role of Mainstream Services*. London: National Children's Bureau.

Special Educational Needs and Disability Act (SENDA) (2001). Norwich: The Stationery Office.

Vernon, J. (1999) *Parent Partnership and SEN: Perspectives on Developing Good Practice*. DfEE Research Report RR162. Nottingham: DfEE Publications.

Vincent, C. (2000) *Including Parents? Education, Citizenship and Parental Agency*. Buckingham: Open University Press.

Warnock, M. (Chair) (1978) *Special Educational Needs*. Norwich: Stationery Office.

White, M. (1997) 'A review of the influence and effects of portage', Chapter 2 in Wolfendale, S. (ed.) *Working with Parents of SEN Children after the Code of Practice*. London: David Fulton Publishers.

Wolfendale, S. (1992) *Empowering Parents and Teachers – For Children*. London: Cassell.

Wolfendale, S. (ed.) (1997) *Working with Parents of SEN Children after the Code of Practice*. London: David Fulton Publishers.

Wolfendale, S. (1999) ' "Parents as Partners" in research and evaluation: methodological and ethical issues and solutions', *British Journal of Special Education*, **26**(3), September, 164–8.

Wolfendale, S. (2001) 'An interim review of the Parent Partnership Service in the London Borough of Sutton', unpublished report, Education Department, London Borough Sutton.

Wolfendale, S. and Bastiani, J. (eds) (2000) *The Contribution of Parents to School Effectiveness*. London: David Fulton Publishers.

Wolfendale, S. and Cook, G. (1997) *Evaluation of SEN Parent Partnership Schemes*. DfEE Research Report No. 34. Nottingham: DfEE Publications.

Wolfendale, S. and Einzig, H. (eds) (1999) *Parenting Education and Support: New Opportunities*. London: David Fulton Publishers.

Chapter 2

Disability rights in education: challenges and opportunities in the SEN and Disability Act 2001

Philippa Russell

Introduction

The SEN and Disability Act 2001 has major implications for education services. The Act not only requires all LEAs to provide Parent Partnership Services and arrangements for mediation, but also amends the Disability Discrimination Act 1995 and introduces disability rights into education. The SEN and Disability Act 2001 will be implemented in September 2002, with accompanying Codes of Practice from the Disability Rights Commission on the school stages of education and post-16 provision for disabled students. The DfES is issuing Planning Guidance to enable schools and LEAs to carry out new duties to plan progressively to improve access to education for disabled pupils (access covering the curriculum, the physical environment and information). A reconstituted SEN and Disability Tribunal will hear cases relating to the disability duties in the school stages of education. The new arrangements have considerable implications for Parent Partnership Services and the voluntary sector, as well as for schools and LEAs.

Background to the SEN and Disability Act 2001

This Government is committed to achieving comprehensive and enforceable rights for disabled people. Our concern is about raising awareness of the contribution that disabled people can and do make at all levels of society. Across Government we are working hard to create a positive climate for disabled people. But legislation on its own is not enough. If we want a fair, modern and inclusive society where everyone is treated with equal respect, then we must allow those talents and ambitions [of disabled people] to be realised. For this reason we accept the recommendations of the Disability Rights Task Force and see equalisation of opportunity for disabled students in education as a high priority.

(David Blunkett, launching the report of the Disability Rights Task Force, 1999)

The Disability Discrimination Act 1995 represented both decades of debate by disabled people and a sea change in government thinking about the need to end discrimination against disabled people and to secure their maximum access and inclusion in community life. However, there was widespread concern that education was excluded from the new legislation. The exclusion of education reflected widespread belief at the time that the effective implementation of the Education Act 1993 and the SEN Code of Practice could be damaged by parallel disability rights legislation and that disabled pupils would be better served through the SEN route. The Disability Rights Commission was established in April 2000 and the government immediately determined that education should now be brought within disability rights legislation in order to end the anomalies and barriers to education experienced by many disabled students. It was acknowledged that the current SEN framework could not comprehensively address all the issues concerning disability discrimination in education and that there were important strategic planning duties for disability for schools and LEAs which needed to be addressed in order to improve access and inclusion.

Following the publication of a consultation paper on the best way forward, the SEN and Disability Act 2001 was given Royal Assent in June 2001, with an implementation date of September 2002. It has been widely welcomed and received cross-party support as it went through Parliament. The new legislation has the potential to bring significant improvements in the educational opportunities available to pupils with SEN and disabilities. It will affect LEAs, schools, including independent and non-maintained special schools, early years providers as well as youth services, further and higher education.

The SEN and Disability Act has two separate parts. The first part amends Part IV of the Education Act 1996 and relates to all children with SEN. The second part amends the Disability Discrimination Act 1995 and brings new requirements to end discrimination against disabled pupils or students into all education services. The first part of the Act applies to England and Wales only. The second part (setting out the disability duties) applies to England, Scotland and Wales. The implementation of the new legislation in September 2002 will be accompanied by two Codes of Practice, explaining the new duties in the school and post-16 stages of education, together with Planning Guidance from the DfES. The new legislation, Codes and related guidance will complement the revised SEN Code of Practice, which was implemented in January 2002.

Special Educational Needs

The SEN and Disability Act makes a number of important amendments to the 1996 Education Act, in particular amending Section 316 of that Act to change the conditions that currently limit the LEA's duty to provide a mainstream place to children with SEN. All LEAs are now required to provide and advertise Parent Partnership Services and must make new arrangements for resolving disputes between parents and schools or LEAs, without affecting parents' right of appeal to the SEN Tribunal. Schools, like parents, will have the same right as parents to request a statutory assessment. They also have a new requirement to inform parents when they make any special educational provision because they have identified their child as having SEN.

Ending disability discrimination in education

On 2 July 2001 the Disability Rights Commission (DRC) issued two draft Codes of Practice on the implications of the disability duties in the SEN and Disability Act 2001. The two Codes of Practice explain:

- the new disability discrimination duties towards disabled children and young people under the SEN and Disability Act 2001 to schools, LEAs and early years providers; and
- the new duties on further and higher education and the youth service towards disabled students in the post-16 stage of education.

As noted above, when the Disability Discrimination Act was passed in 1995, education was exempted from its provisions (though other providers of goods and services have been covered since 1996). In 1997 the new government sought the advice of the Disability Rights Task Force (DRTF) on how disability discrimination duties should be extended to cover education. The DRTF gave powerful messages about the need to introduce disability rights into education, drawing upon the success of IDEA (the Individuals with Disabilities Education Act) in the USA in doing the following:

- addressing the social exclusion and disadvantage which characterise the lives of too many disabled people;
- recognising the importance of building strong strategic partnerships with schools and LEAs, with a focus on planned

progression towards greater access and inclusion within the education system;

- ensuring as far as possible that any new disability rights in education are dovetailed with the existing SEN Framework, to avoid parallel systems.

The new duties focus quite specifically on protecting pupils and potential pupils from discrimination on the grounds of disability. The duties assume that special educational provision for disabled children and young people is made through the special educational needs route, and that physical access needs will be met through longer-term and more strategic planning duties for schools and for LEAs, which will come into effect in September 2002. The new legislation and its related Codes of Practice and Planning Guidance offer both challenges and opportunities for Parent Partnership Services, which will now need to address a wider range of issues relating to disabled children and in particular to the broader definition of 'education and associated services' for disabled children.

Who is disabled within the new legislation?

Many (but not all) disabled children will also have special educational needs and thereby be covered by the existing SEN Frameworks in England, Wales and Scotland. The definition of disability with reference to the new duties towards 'disabled' pupils in education is that used in the Disability Discrimination Act 1995. This definition says that: 'a person has a disability if he or she has a physical or mental impairment that has a substantial and long-term adverse effect on his or her ability to carry out normal day-to-day activities'. The term 'impairment' covers physical or learning disabilities; sensory impairments such as those affecting sight or hearing; mental health problems and specific conditions such as HIV, cancer or other clinically recognised illnesses *if* (in all cases) they meet the test of 'substantial and long-term adverse effects'. The definition could include children with emotional and behavioural difficulties or dyslexia and similar conditions if the effect of the impairment is sufficiently 'adverse and severe'.

There is some anecdotal evidence from Australia and the USA, which have similar legislation, that parents may actively seek the 'dual diagnosis' of SEN and disability in order to utilise disability rights in education. In both the USA and the UK, disability rights in education cover the whole life of the school (i.e. include out-of-school activities such as school trips), whereas the SEN Framework specifically addresses the child's curricular activities.

Who is responsible for implementing the new duties?

The legislation refers to 'the responsible body'. The responsible body will usually be the Governing Body of the school or, if the school is run by the LEA, the local authority itself. In the case of independent or non-maintained schools, the responsible body will be the Board of Management or Governing Body (however described). The responsible body has a corporate responsibility for ensuring that the disability duties are carried across all aspects of school life. Therefore, if a teacher acts in a discriminatory way or if the school permits a private contractor to run an after-school activity which discriminates against disabled pupils, the school's Governing or 'responsible' body will be collectively responsible in most cases. Hence all education providers must have regard to all aspects of the life of their school, to ensure that there is no less favourable treatment for disabled pupils and that reasonable adjustments have been made as appropriate.

Key duties in ensuring that education services do not discriminate against disabled pupils

There are two key duties in the new legislation, namely:

- not to treat disabled pupils less favourably for a reason that relates to their disability; and
- to make reasonable adjustments in order to ensure that disabled pupils are not at a substantial disadvantage.

As noted above, the new duties cover every aspect of the life of the school: from teaching and learning to after-school clubs; from school organisation to what happens in the dinner queue; from timetabling to the use of classroom support; from homework to anti-bullying policies; from admissions to exclusions. In considering how they may prevent discrimination against disabled pupils, all education providers (including those working in the early years) must have regard to the following:

- access to the physical environment;
- access to the curriculum;
- the provision of information in accessible formats.

In particular, the new duties specifically apply to:

- admissions;
- education and associated services;
- exclusions.

However, the reasonable adjustments duties do not require the 'responsible body':

- to provide auxiliary aids and equipment (i.e. it is assumed that the SEN statutory route will be used for specific pieces of equipment or aids);
- to make physical alterations to the physical features of the school.

Some education providers have been confused by the general duties to improve access to the physical environment and the exemption of physical adaptations from those duties. They need to understand that physical alterations to schools are not required under the reasonable adjustments duty as it is anticipated that these will be achieved through a longer-term and more strategic approach to improving access to school buildings (i.e. through the planning duties). Hence all education providers should be anticipating the Planning Guidance and the requirement for schools to have accessibility plans and for LEAs to have accessibility strategies. Within these new planning arrangements, schools and other providers will need to demonstrate that they are anticipating and planning for the needs of disabled pupils and thereby progressively improving access through refurbishment programmes and other activities. They will need to remember that both current disabled pupils and prospective disabled pupils are covered by the new duties.

Admissions arrangements

Schools, early years providers and LEAs must take steps to ensure that they do not discriminate against disabled pupils in admission arrangements through:

- refusing or deliberately omitting to accept an application for admission from a disabled pupil;
- the terms on which they are willing to admit a disabled pupil;
- criteria used for admission (for example, when the school is over-subscribed).

Exclusions

The new duties also make it unlawful for a responsible body to discriminate against a disabled pupil by excluding him or her from the school for a reason related to the pupil's disability for which there is no 'justification'. These duties apply whether the exclusion is permanent or for a fixed term.

What are 'education and associated services'?

'Education and associated services' is a broad term that covers all aspects of school life. It may include:

- access to the curriculum;
- teaching and learning (including classroom organisation);
- timetabling and grouping of pupils;
- activities to supplement the curriculum, such as school trips, theatre visits, etc.;
- school policies;
- school sports, leisure and cultural activities;
- assessment and examination arrangements;
- school discipline and sanctions.

In some areas of school life, the duties on the responsible bodies will overlap with other duties on other services (for example, providers of health services). Other non-educational agencies already have duties not to discriminate against disabled people under Part III of the Disability Discrimination Act 1995.

What is discrimination and less favourable treatment?

Part IV of the Disability Discrimination Act 1995, as amended by the SEN and Disability Act 2001, makes it unlawful for a responsible body for a school to discriminate against a disabled child in relation to his or her access to education. Discrimination against a disabled child in education can occur in two possible ways. Discrimination is either:

- treating a disabled pupil or prospective pupil less favourably for a reason relating to his or her disability than someone to whom that reason does not apply, without justification; or
- failing to make reasonable adjustments to admission arrange- ments or education and associated services, without which adjustments a disabled pupil would be placed at a 'substantial disadvantage' in comparison with his/her non-disabled peers (unless there is a justification for failing to make such an adjustment).

These two duties are at the core of the new arrangements. For 'less favourable treatment' to be invoked, there are three tests:

- the less favourable treatment is related to the child's disability;
- the disabled child is being treated less favourably than someone without a disability;
- there is no justification for the different or less favourable treatment.

The DRC Code of Practice on the school stages of education gives detailed guidance with practical illustrations of how the definitions of less favourable treatment and reasonable adjustments might be applied.

An example of the new duties could be as set out below:

> Peter has been refused admission to a secondary school, which has a specialism in music. He has met the musical criteria for admission to the school and the school is fully accessible, thereby able to meet his access needs. However, he has epilepsy and the school argues that it cannot accommodate his special needs with regard to this condition and the administration of his medication.

In this case, Peter is likely to have received less favourable treatment, for which there is no justification. He meets the criteria for admission to a school with a music specialism (i.e. he complies with the 'permitted form of selection' allowed under the SEN and Disability Act). He will have no access problems at the school, which has been the subject of a major refurbishment and access initiative. While teaching staff cannot be legally required to administer medication unless they choose to do, no assessment has been made of *when* Peter requires such medication (in fact, he takes it at home) nor of the likely incidence of his fits. Peter's medication is in fact well controlled and his paediatrician supports his application. This is likely to be a case of 'less favourable treatment'. The school has refused Peter's admission for no justifiable reason. They have failed to assess his support needs or to consider how they might meet such needs and have thereby made unreasonable presumptions about his unsuitability for the placement in question.

Information sharing and confidentiality

In Peter's case, the LEA and school have information from a variety of sources about Peter's disability. It is very clear what access and other needs will be required if he attends a particular school. But what would happen if the disability is 'hidden' and the family prefer not to disclose it to the school?

> Chloe has poorly controlled diabetes and has started at a new school. She is 11 years old. She needs to carry biscuits to eat when her blood sugar drops. Her parents are determined not to tell the school about her disability and she is similarly forbidden to mention it. She attends one class and needs to eat a biscuit. The teacher in question has a strict 'no eating' policy in her class and the biscuits are confiscated. Chloe has a hypoglycaemic attack and has to go to hospital. The parents argue that the school has discriminated against her by removing the biscuits and thereby forcing the family to acknowledge her condition.

Information sharing between parents, pupils and teachers is obviously very relevant to positive approaches to access and inclusion. But there is no onus on parents and pupils to share this information, if they wish to keep it confidential. However, if the school cannot anticipate a pupil's special needs without such information, then it may be able to claim that it acted reasonably because it had no way of knowing about the child's disability. But, if Chloe had told anyone at the school for example, the school secretary – that she had diabetes – then the school could be held responsible for not sharing relevant information. In the circumstances, the school is likely to have acted reasonably because of a lack of knowledge defence. But it would be good practice for schools to encourage information sharing (particularly concerning admissions to the school) as a positive step in meeting the needs of all pupils.

Schools (and other education providers, for example, independent schools and early years providers) should be aware of the importance of seeing the duty to make reasonable adjustments as being anticipatory and not only concerning the circumstances of a particular disabled child.

Schools will need to review all their policies, practices and procedures to ensure that they do not discriminate against disabled pupils who might come to the school in the future, by putting them at a substantial disadvantage. The new Planning Guidance will provide a framework for thinking strategically about promoting access and avoiding discrimination. But schools should already be thinking about disability equality training and ensuring that their SEN policies are 'disability friendly'. They should also remember that positive and creative attitudes towards inclusion will overcome many barriers. As one school noted (personal communication):

Anticipating the SEN and Disability Act and wishing to improve access and inclusion in a rural school with a wide catchment area and limited choice of alternatives, we invited a local organisation of disabled people to carry out an access audit and to set us short-, medium- and long-term targets. We have used our refurbishment budget well; we have found that many improvements can be made for minimal cost and, very importantly, we have involved the whole community.

Making our school more accessible has had unexpected 'pluses'. Our chair of governors was injured in a car accident and was a wheelchair user for four months. We depend on her and she was able to visit us as usual! Two of our children and a parent also had mobility problems because of illness or accidents. Nobody had to stay away. We also realised that access is not only about the physical environment. We have examined all our activities, from the core curriculum to our local drama group and our sporting and other activities. By anticipating and not waiting for the first disabled child to appear, we have all benefited. We have also benefited financially because our now accessible school can be hired out for a range of community activities!

Schools should be aware that if they let or loan premises for non-educational activities (e.g. for sport or for evening clubs or classes), then they are automatically covered by Part III of the Disability Discrimination Act and *must* comply with its requirements with reference to access to goods and services.

Dispute resolution: means of redress

Part I of the SEN and Disability Act 2001 introduces new mediation arrangements for disputes concerning special educational needs. Parents will retain the right to take their case to the Tribunal if they choose to go down the mediation route.

Parents of disabled children who think that their child has been discriminated against can make a claim of disability discrimination on behalf of their disabled child to the re-named SEN and Disability Tribunal, which will have an extended role to hear disability cases. Any claim of discrimination on grounds of disability will be made against the 'responsible body' for the school or education service in question. In most circumstances this will be the governing body of the school, though in some circumstances it is the local education authority.

The Disability Rights Commission will provide a conciliation service for disability rights in education disputes and parents and schools should be aware that the Commission also provides a Help Line (08457 622633) and case work service which, from September 2002, can cover educational as well as other disputes.

Victimisation

Victimisation is a special form of discrimination covered by the Disability Discrimination Act 1995. It applies whether or not the person victimised is a disabled person.

James has noticed that Sally, a disabled pupil in his class, is regularly excluded from classroom activities and is sometimes teased by one of the classroom assistants. The same assistant frequently blocks Sally from sitting at the front of the class so that she can see the board clearly and does not always give her the homework notes in a large font to take home. Sally and her parents make a complaint, but are told that her behaviour is bad and she is at fault. James agrees to support the complaint, but is subsequently excluded from a school play and dropped from the football team without explanation.

James is likely to have been discriminated against and treated less favourably, because he has supported a disabled pupil. Parents and siblings are also protected from victimisation if they have, for example, made a complaint or supported a complaint or brought other proceedings under the Act.

Accessibility plans and accessibility strategies

As noted above, the new requirements are anticipatory. Hence high quality strategic planning will be crucial for effective implementation. The Planning Guidance to accompany the legislation and Codes of Practice will require schools and LEAs to prepare a plan or strategy to increase, over time, the physical accessibility of the school environment and the curriculum for both current and future pupils. The planning arrangements must also include arrangements to improve the communication of information for disabled pupils. Independent and non-maintained schools must also produce plans or strategies and in all cases the planning arrangements must be kept under review and be regularly revised. The plans are expected to be realistic and to take account of the existing resources (and barriers) of the school in question. But the new planning arrangements must be more than 'paper exercises'. There will be a duty to implement plans and strategies and they will be inspected by Ofsted.

Implications for the future – a new and extended role for Parent Partnership Services

Parent Partnership Services, in fulfilling their broader roles and responsibilities as set out in the revised SEN Code of Practice and within the SEN and Disability Act and its related guidance, will have important roles not in only supporting individual parents and children in dispute resolution but hopefully in:

- Working more broadly with 'whole schools' to assist and advise them in considering how they can promote greater access to the life of the school (with special reference to accessibility plans).
- Ensuring that parents (and disabled children) can provide relevant information to support a child's inclusion in a school or after-school activity and that schools have access to disability equality training which creates positive expectations rather than anxieties about health and safety issues or inaccurate presumptions about the negative consequences of a particular disability.
- Ensuring that there are sufficient Independent Parental Supporters with disability equality training, who can not only

provide practical advice and support on SEN issues, but who are also familiar with the new disability rights in education and can provide accurate and relevant advice to parents and to schools.

- Encouraging multi-agency partnerships (particularly in early years and transition planning), recognising that, for many disabled pupils, additional support and advice may be needed from child health or social services departments.
- Providing relevant information for parents and schools not only on the educational implications of a particular disability but also on the practical management of that disability in a variety of educational settings.
- Working with the independent and non-maintained sector with special reference to early years provision and non-maintained or independent residential schools. Parent Partnership Services, in general, have had little contact with the independent or non-maintained sectors, or (in most parts of the country) with early years services. The application of the new disability duties to both these sectors mean that parents (and providers) will be looking for information and advice, which Parent Partnership Services may be well equipped to provide.
- Encouraging young disabled people to play a more pro-active role in clarifying their own access needs and in negotiating access to the wider range of activities, which form the basis of school life.
- Encouraging local disability and parent organisations to work together with schools and the LEA so that accessibility plans for schools (and accessibility strategies for LEAs) reflect both local needs and set realistic targets. Many schools may be unaware that the Disability Rights Commission is much more than an enforcement body and can provide practical help and advice. The Commission will be producing good practice guidance (a toolkit to access and inclusion) to accompany its Codes and wishes to have a pro-active role in working in partnership with schools as well as the voluntary sector to implement the new legislation in as strategic a way as possible.

The new duties raise important issues about the following:

- the need for a corporate and 'whole school' responsibility for preventing disability discrimination;
- the importance of clear strategic planning to promote access and inclusion. Education services have an anticipatory duty towards disabled pupils, as well as duties not to discriminate against individual children and young people;

- the need for staff training and professional development on disability equality issues;
- the quality of information provided to parents on the support which schools can offer disabled pupils. The new disability duties expect that such information will be provided in an accessible format;
- the need to improve in-school as well as statutory assessment of disabled pupils to ensure that any special needs related specifically to their disability are clearly addressed. In the USA, amendments to IDEA (Individuals with Disabilities Education Act 1997) require schools and Education Departments to include a 'disability impact statement' within pupils' Individual Education Plans to ensure that they are not disadvantaged in their access to the full life of the school.

Although some schools have been initially alarmed at the new duties, many recognise that they are already making positive adjustments to meet the needs of all members of the school community! The test of what is reasonable will always apply. The duties in the Act are anticipatory and schools and LEAs and Education Departments will have new planning guidance (to be implemented in September 2002) on 'thinking access and inclusion' in a strategic and realistic way. New funding is available through an enhanced Schools Access Initiative in England and Wales. Schools in England and Wales will be required to have accessibility plans, LEAs will be required to have accessibility strategies. Both will be inspected by Ofsted.

The consultation paper on Education (Disability Strategies and Pupils' Records) (Scotland) Bill (2001) sets out the proposed arrangements in Scotland for schools to prepare and implement strategies relating to the accessibility of school education and educational records for pupils. In considering what 'reasonable steps' they should take to avoid discrimination, schools will have to have regard to the DRC Code of Practice.

An important first step will therefore be ensuring that all planning arrangements in the school take account of the needs of current and prospective disabled pupils. For example, refurbishment plans offer good opportunities to upgrade the physical environment of the school. The SEN policy should already address the needs of disabled pupils.

Because equal opportunities legislation remains a Westminster responsibility, the new disability duties apply throughout England, Wales and Scotland. They apply to all schools, whether independent or maintained, mainstream or special, nursery, primary or secondary, community, voluntary, foundation or a city academy.

The new duties are explained in the DRC Code of Practice. As noted above, the Draft Code of Practice was published on 2 July 2001 and the consultation ran until 31 October 2001. The SEN and Disability Act 2001, related regulations and planning guidance and the Code of Practice will be implemented in September 2002.

References

Disability Rights Commission (2001) *Schools Code of Practice – SEN and Disability Act.* London: DfES.

Disability Rights Commission (2001) *Post-16 Code of Practice – SEN and Disability Act.* London: DfES.

Disability Rights Task Force (1999) *From Exclusion to Inclusion: A Report of the DRTF on Civil Rights for Disabled People.* London: DfES.

Chapter 3

The development of the National Parent Partnership Network

Philippa Stobbs

Introduction

The National Parent Partnership Network is a network that brings together all the Parent Partnership Services across the country, including a number of voluntary organisations that are funded by local education authorities to provide information and support to parents. The Network is supported by a small allocation of staffing from the Council for Disabled Children. The Council has been funded by the Department for Education and Skills since 1995 to provide this support to the Network and to meet the Department's own need for information about services.

There have been distinctive periods in partnership with parents and hence in the role of those supporting the services that are working directly with parents. This chapter has a narrative running through it, following the development of services through these different periods, and the role of the Council in supporting them. Woven into the narrative is a discussion of some of the issues that have been the focus of much of the debate about parent partnership and that have provided fertile territory for the development of the Network.

Support for parents, BC

The support provided by the Council for Disabled Children (the Council) to the network of Parent Partnership Services across the country has its origins in two main areas: the nature of the Council itself; and the work of the Council through the 1980s and early 1990s. This is the period referred to here as BC, that is, Before the Code of Practice.

The Council for Disabled Children is an independently elected Council established under the auspices of the National Children's Bureau. It has representation from parents, voluntary organisations, professional associations and statutory agencies. Its aim is to identify gaps and overlaps in the provision of services to children with special educational needs and disabilities, to support the development of policy and practice, and to work with national and local government to improve services. It is uniquely placed to bring different parties together to identify ways in which services can better meet the needs of children and young people with special educational needs and disabilities and their families.

Over different eras in parent partnership work the Council has been involved in highlighting to government both the difficulties experienced by parents and possible ways forward for national and local policy and practice. During the passage of the Education Act 1981 the Council (then the Voluntary Council for Handicapped Children) argued for information and support for parents whose children were going through the process of statutory assessment. As a last minute addition the Act included the requirement to provide parents with a Named Person.

The Council played an important part in promoting a debate about the role of the Named Person (Russell 1983) but at this stage there was no funding to support the development of these ideas. To the extent that the role of the Named Person did develop through the 1980s and early 1990s, it was very much through the work of voluntary organisations.

The need for such work was great. Reports throughout the 1980s documented the failure of the procedures under the 1981 Act to operate in the intended spirit of partnership (GLAD 1988; Berridge and Russell 1988). The House of Commons Education, Science and Arts Select Committee (1987) concluded that, in respect of partnership with parents and in many other ways, the 1981 Act was 'not working satisfactorily'.

During the passage of the 1993 Act and the subsequent drafting of the first Code of Practice (DfE 1994) with its strong emphasis on active support for parents, the Council had argued that it was timely to reconsider the role of the Named Person. Late in the day the Named Person and Parent Partnership Schemes were written into the Code of Practice and central government funding was allocated to promote their development.

Over two rounds of legislation, the Council had argued strongly for the development of a closer partnership between parents and professionals and for the development of information and support for parents. In particular, the Council had argued for the implementation of the Named Person. It was a combination of a national political voice, the ability to bring together key information, and the ability to support development work, combined with the nature of the Council itself that were crucial elements in the Council's role in the post-Code era in the development of partnership with parents.

The post-Code era

In the months following the publication of the Code of Practice, and with a supported grant from central government in the form of Grants for Education Support and Training (GEST), local education authorities started to establish Parent Partnership Schemes. The first Parent Partnership Officers (PPO) were appointed but schemes were by and large viewed by LEAs as a temporary measure and, in some places, there was little commitment to schemes beyond the GEST-funded year. More LEAs began to appoint Parent Partnership Officers when, towards the end of 1994, supported grant for a second year was assured in the DFE Circular setting out the GEST arrangements for 1995–96. While some LEAs were slow off the mark, there were others who had Parent Partnership Officers in post in April 1994 and some who established their parent partnership post as a permanent post from the outset.

Whatever their circumstances, Parent Partnership Schemes developed rapidly, The Wolfendale and Cook research (1997) shows that the early focus of the schemes was very much on the development of information for parents and the recruitment, training and support of Named Persons. A range of further issues also set challenges for schemes in their early development and set an agenda for the dialogue that developed within the network of schemes.

The National Parent Partnership Network was formed, in part, to facilitate this dialogue. The Council had written to the DFE proposing a consortium to support Parent Partnership Schemes in the development of positive partnership between parents, schools, LEAs and the voluntary sector. The consortium aimed to do the following:

- encourage schemes to learn from each other;
- share information;
- reduce duplication of effort;
- describe interesting and innovative work.

The Council also saw this as an opportunity to address a national agenda that had been developing and risked undermining the positive benefits of the introduction of Parent Partnership Schemes. While there had been a general welcome for the establishment of schemes, there were also tensions both nationally and locally about the respective roles of the voluntary sector and LEA-funded schemes in the provision of information and support for parents. In establishing the Network, the Council wanted to address this tension. A steering group for the project brought together voluntary sector expertise and representatives of LEAs, who, with the support of the DFE through the

GEST scheme, now held the money and were charged with the development of Parent Partnership work. From the beginning the steering group also included a number of serving PPOs. The steering group for the Network developed primarily as a forum in which national policy for special educational needs and disability issues could be discussed in relation to parent support work and a positive dialogue could be established between the voluntary and statutory sectors on parent partnership issues.

The practical work of support to the Network got under way during 1995. The means by which the Council sought to address the broad aims which it had proposed were set out in the first newsletter:

CDC has been funded by the Department for Education and Employment for a year to:

- develop an information base of interesting and innovative practice on all aspects of working with parents and parent organisations so that a range of different approaches can be shared with others;
- identify issues which are causing doubt and concern and work towards their solution;
- draw together existing training materials and recruitment strategies for Named Persons;
- share experiences of the effectiveness of different ways of working.

We plan to do this with a series of seminars and workshops, with factsheets and this newsletter, by visiting projects and attending regional conferences.

(NPPN Newsletter, October 1995)

The Director of the Council had oversight of the Council's work in support of the Network; an information officer was recruited to develop the database and the collection of materials – this was five days a month of a post that was allocated across a number of different projects; a development officer was allocated, three days a month, to other duties including the editing of the newsletter and the other materials produced by and for the Network; and a small amount of administrative support was allocated to the production and circulation of the newsletters and other materials.

The first challenge for the Council was to find out who was in post and where. The DfEE provided some contacts, some PPOs got in touch with the Council, others were contacted through regional events. Lines of communication were gradually established, but in some cases the first newsletter and accompanying papers, October 1995, had to be sent to the host LEAs.

Gradually, schemes provided information for the database outlining the main areas of their work. By July 1966, there was information entered for 80 per cent of LEAs. Ultimately, there were some LEAs who did not send any information and some of these never established a Parent Partnership Scheme as such. That would have to wait until a statutory requirement was imminent.

At a time of exponential increase in the storage of and access to electronic information, it is hard to remember how innovative the database itself was at this stage. It was sufficiently novel that a demonstration was organised for the Department for Education and Employment.

The information that had been brought together on the database, along with the accompanying literature in the growing resource collection, was used in a wide variety of ways:

- to facilitate contact between parent partnership officers;
- to put parents . . . in touch with the relevant parent partnership staff in their local education authority;
- to enable newly appointed parent partnership officers . . . to draw on database information and accompanying literature as part of the induction process to the post;
- to provide relevant information for LEAs, voluntary organisations . . . and others on a range of issues relating to parent partnership;
- to aid researchers in their studies.

(CDC 1996)

The database itself helped in identifying interesting and innovative approaches to Parent Partnership work, as did contact with schemes and with the regional groups that had started to meet. Newsletters, 'Information exchanges' (analyses of the approaches that schemes were adopting in relation to particular issues), training days and Council attendance at local, regional and national events were all vehicles for the dissemination of the information gathered. In addition the Council supported and promoted research work, providing access for researchers to all its records and ensuring a platform for the discussion of their findings.

The newsletters provided for an exchange of more personal accounts of developments, the opportunity to advertise materials and events, and for communication about national policy. In the first three newsletters the majority of items were focused on practice development. What is remarkable about these contributions is the insights they provide into the rapid development of the schemes at this stage. Typically, schemes started with a desk, a phone and a copy of the Code. Some schemes started with the additional benefit of background research into parents' views. All were focused on the key task of establishing systems for providing information and support to parents with a sense of urgency that may have been partly induced by the knowledge that, for many schemes, their continued existence beyond April 1997 was not assured.

Through their enquiries, their expressions of interest and concern, PPOs identified the selection of topics that needed to be addressed in the newsletters. Much of the interesting and innovative practice had to be sought out. Typically, PPOs did not see that they were doing anything remarkable. Aspects of the work that were addressed in the newsletters in the first year were:

- a range of approaches to the recruitment, training and support of Named Persons;
- support to parents of bilingual children;
- working with schools and with parents at Stages 1–3 of the Code of Practice;
- the monitoring and evaluation of schemes.

In this first period of Parent Partnership Schemes, the cessation of GEST funding was always just around the corner and the Council promoted monitoring and evaluation as the focus for an early 'Information exchange'. Monitoring and evaluation had been selected in order to support schemes in considering how they might collect together evidence to argue for their continued existence after GEST funding. At the time the information was first drawn together many schemes undertook routine monitoring but only a few, in fact three, had undertaken a full evaluation. Six months later, when the information was updated, four more schemes had been evaluated and two more were in the pipeline. The focus on particular aspects of Parent Partnership work could be re-emphasised by ensuring there were articles in the newsletter and sessions on training days addressing these same issues.

The Council collected and organised information but also disseminated it in a range of different ways, to a range of others including parents, voluntary organisations, researchers and schemes themselves. The Council also played a part in promoting discussion and highlighting innovative practice in particular areas of Parent Partnership work.

The resource collection developed rapidly as materials were produced by schemes. The collection was invaluable for the induction of new PPOs, but, based at the National Children's Bureau, it was also available to a wide range of others with an interest in the area.

At this stage the focus of most of the dialogue within the Network was on practice issues. There was quite a lot of counting of schemes, but there was little discussion of national policy, with the notable exception of funding. To support schemes in arguing for their continued existence, the Council circulated information about the GEST allocations made to individual LEAs. Equally, funding was the only aspect of national policy discussed in the newsletter. There was one item on this, namely the news, July 1886, that GEST funding of Parent Partnership Schemes would cease in April 1997.

The wilderness year

Thus, 1997–98 was a difficult year for many schemes. Within the cessation of GEST money in April 1997, the year started with many schemes being wound up. Some Parent Partnership Officers who left their posts at this stage were simply not replaced. In other LEAs, seconded officers returned to their previous posts. Some LEAs tried, through other means, to maintain support for parents. Some LEAs started to include responsibility for Parent Partnership into other posts. Other schemes drew on information they had collected through monitoring and evaluation activities to point to their effectiveness and argue for their continuation. The Council sought out information and circulated it regularly.

The greatest concern was for those areas where posts were lost. The impact on parents locally was significant and left volunteer parents feeling angry. Unsupported, they became the only contact point for other parents. Their phones did not stop ringing, 'it affects the whole family, they all take messages' (Henderson 1998) and, understandably, they felt resentful.

Some schemes sought to establish themselves as separate organis-ations with charitable status. Some schemes advocated this route as providing them with the independence that they wanted:

> independence allows us to set our own work priorities and work direction;
> independence means that we no longer need to follow the LEA line;
> independence is seen as a positive asset by the parents we help;
> independence allows us to work with all the relevant statutory bodies, not just the LEA;
> independence allows consultation and partnership with the LEA, building on previously nurtured contacts.
>
> (Hunt and Magee 1998)

However, the disadvantages were also recognised:

> lack of funding;
> not being able to influence LEA policy and practice from within.
>
> (Ibid.)

The Wolfendale and Cook research was completed in July 1997 and the report was published by the DfEE in the autumn. The report provided good arguments for the continuation of Parent Partnership Schemes but did not stop some of them disappearing.

By the autumn of 1997 the new government had published its Green Paper with its promise of a long-term commitment to working in partnership with parents. There was also the promise of reviving central support from April 1998, through the newly established Standards Fund. However, with tight spending controls on education at this stage, many LEAs were uncertain about their ability to raise their share of the funding. By March 1998 there were signs of both further decline and new hope.

The positive outcomes from this year included the recognition by some LEAs of the deleterious impact on schemes of having to negotiate for their existence every year and of the consequent lack of security for staff. Recognising this, a number of LEAs established their Parent Partnership posts as 'permanent' posts.

In supporting the Network in this phase, the Council continued to bring together and disseminate information in a variety of ways: through training days, newsletters, information exchanges on a range of different aspects of practice. The Council also had an increasing role in actively promoting parent partnership work nationally, regionally and locally. Nationally, the Council promoted parent partnership work through the wide variety of networks linked to the Council, by writing about schemes for a range of publications, and by developing a national voice on policy with government. Council representation on a number of national bodies enabled it to argue the case for Parent Partnership Schemes and to raise awareness of the work.

The Council also visited a number of regional events, sometimes providing a national perspective for promotional events, at other times joining the developing regional discussions. There was a growing number of ways in which the Council was providing support to individual schemes: through the provision of information and advice, through speaking at local events, contributing to extended training opportunities, and, when it was sought, through support to individual LEAs in planning how best to deploy and/or develop their Parent Partnership Service.

The Standards Fund, from April 1998

A word about language. The Government's Programme of Action (DfEE 1998) made a commitment to a statutory requirement on LEAs to provide a Parent Partnership Service. Round about this time the word 'scheme' with all its connotations of short-term arrangements was increasingly replaced by the word 'service' which conveyed a message of greater permanence, of a longer-term commitment. Similarly, the title 'Parent Partnership Officer' was gradually replaced by the title 'Parent Partnership Coordinator'. This was perhaps in part to put some distance between the role of an LEA officer and the person leading the Parent Partnership Service, but also to reflect the changing nature of the work, increasingly that of coordinating a range of activities.

Government policy and the Network

This was a time of rapid development of government policy. In early 1999, the Council organised two consultative days for Parent Partnership Coordinators. The first focused on the Programme of Action, the second on the proposed revision of the 1994 Code of Practice. During these events services started to consider what the key elements of parent partnership work were. If Parent Partnership Services were to become a statutory requirement, what would constitute a service? How would anyone know if the LEA had met the requirement? What evidence would there need to be? The discussions on these key questions formed one of the starting points for new work on standards which later fed in to the revision of the Code of Practice, the SEN Toolkit and the work of the Network on a Practice Guide for Parent Partnership Services.

Another element in government policy was the commitment to mediation. This commitment stemmed, at least in part, from concerns that, over the years since the establishment of the SEN Tribunal, approximately half of all appeals had been withdrawn before they were heard. By definition, these were disputes that were capable of resolution.

Within the Network there had always been an interest in mediation. There was obvious common ground between the processes at work in parent partnership and in mediation. At the same time there were questions about whether Parent Partnership Coordinators could become mediators. In circumstances where they had been involved in supporting the parents, could they subsequently act as a neutral third party? The Council arranged some intensive training to enable everyone to develop a better understanding of mediation.

Those who attended the training came to an appreciation of the very specific skills required for mediation and an appreciation of the complexity of the infrastructure needed to support mediation. This helped to clarify, first, whether or not they might go further and develop mediation skills themselves and, second, how the Parent Partnership Service might support the development of local arrangements.

The Council brought together an information exchange on the mediation arrangements that were developing nationally. The response showed that some LEAs simply expected their Parent Partnership Service to provide mediation. In other LEAs mediation expertise was being sought from other fields, such as housing, and imported into education. Some LEAs were working together in consortia to find a larger population base for the provision of mediation services. The Council supported the early development of one of these consortia. The DfES recognised the more appropriate population base of a consortium approach and supported this with £1.5 million channelled through the SEN Regional Partnerships to help develop the independent element in mediation services.

The government had made a clear commitment to the development of partnership with parents and the Council sought to promote an understanding of how that might come about. An important part of the Council's role at this stage was facilitating the voice of Parent Partnership Services in the growing debate about these developments.

The development of the Network

In some LEAs services started to develop very rapidly at this stage. Services developed in a number of ways: they gradually undertook a wider range of activities; increased their staffing; increased their funding but also increased the number of routes through which they secured funding. Overall these services became more complex to manage.

In one LEA the training of Independent Parental Supporters (IPS), who would replace Named Persons, was contracted out to a voluntary organisation. In addition four Parent Partnership assistants were appointed to supplement the role of the Parent Partnership Coordinator. In another LEA, staffing of the service gradually increased from one full-time coordinator in 1996 to a total, in 2001–2, of six staff (4.1 full-time equivalent) including administrative support. The staff are allocated to different areas of work and the funding, which has gradually diversified, now comes from seven different sources.

At the same time other LEAs, at least initially, determined not to provide a service and, for some, where a service had been provided and then withdrawn, there was a partnership deficit that would have to be addressed before positive progress could be made. Thus it was that the variation between services became more pronounced at this stage.

In time it became apparent that the government was determined that there would be a Parent Partnership Service available in every area and gradually new appointments were made. The support needed by these newly appointed coordinators was rather different from what was needed by those in the longer-established services.

Those who were new in post were seeking the induction and information sharing activities that characterised the early stages of the Network. Longer-established services were grappling with Best Value reviews and Ofsted inspections and were looking for support in preparing for these activities. Different training days were arranged to address the different needs.

The training and support needs of the Network were changing in other ways as well. While there was a continuing demand for updates on both policy and practice issues, there was also a growing interest in more extended opportunities for continuing professional development (CPD). A review by the Council showed a particular interest in developing expertise in management and in understanding of the legislation. The Council has started to develop the links that may be helpful in providing these more extended opportunities for professional development.

The growing variation between services at this stage raised questions about what might constitute a Parent Partnership Service if, as anticipated, services became a statutory requirement. Linked to this were questions about how coordinators might set priorities among the many demands on their service, and how they might plan for the development of their service. At the same time a new agenda was developing with Best Value reviews in local authorities. The voluntary sector, too, was beginning to develop standards in services (National Deaf Children's Society 1999).

Around this time the Council secured some funding for a Practice Guide to describe and promote the work of Parent Partnership Services. The Council wanted this guide to be more than an account of the work of services and proposed to structure it around the development of standards for Parent Partnership work.

There were concerns expressed by services that standards that could be achieved in some areas would be unattainable in others. However, there was considerable support from services for a set of standards which, while not being intimidating, should nonetheless be aspirational. Enough work had been done on the standards in time to share drafts with the DfES as the 2001 Code of Practice and the SEN Toolkit were being put together. In consequence, there is much common ground between the Guide and what the Code and the Toolkit say on parent partnership.

Services were now communicating in different ways and asking for different sorts of information. Electronic communication transformed the way information passed around the Network. As the use of email grew the Council worked with BECTa to establish the Virtual Parent Partnership Forum. While there were teething problems with the level and flow of information, the feedback on the use of the Forum has been positive. The Forum is providing an excellent way of keeping

Parent Partnership Coordinators in touch and there have been some good moments when services, sometimes the last to be in the know, received national news on SEN and disability issues before their LEA colleagues. In addition, the Council established the National Parent Partnership Network website and information produced by the Council for the Network is now available there.

Over this period services themselves made a significant contribution to the development of national policy. In the early stages the voice on national policy was facilitated by the Council. It is now a voice that services have in their own right through the National Association of Parent Partnership Services, **napps** (see Chapter 4).

Over this period the Council has increased the representation of Parent Partnership Coordinators on the steering and working groups for the Network, to ensure their involvement in the oversight of the work of the Council, and to ensure that it is responsive to the needs of services. The regional groups are well established and each regional group sends a representative. In addition, the membership of the steering group, which has more of a policy focus, has been updated to reflect the wider range of organisations now involved in Parent Partnership work nationally.

Through all the different eras of Parent Partnership a small but consistent element in the work of the Council has been the provision of support and advice for LEAs in thinking about how to deploy their service. It has sometimes been difficult for LEAs to stand back sufficiently to see how they may reap the benefits of the support that services can provide to parents at the same time as benefiting from the challenge that services can provide to LEAs themselves – the challenge that can inform improvements in the ways in which they work with parents, and ways in which they might develop policy, provision and practice.

A statutory basis for services with national standards

During this period the aims for the Council's support for the Network remained as they had been at the outset, though the objectives for the work have developed over time. The changing nature of services will require changes in the nature of the support provided to them. The Council decided that it was an important moment at which to review the support that the Council provides to the Network.

The review has coincided with a period when the post of co-ordinator is held by an external consultant. This provides the Council with the opportunity to take a more objective look at how it can most usefully plan the longer-term development of its support for the Network. At the same time it will need to seek a more stable funding base with a longer-term commitment to its work. A comparatively small allocation of staffing to the support of the Network and variations in levels of funding have unquestionably caused difficulties in maintaining a consistent service.

In reviewing the support for the Network it is important to consider the ways in which services themselves are changing. Looking to the future: What will the role of Parent Partnership Services be? What support will they most need?

Services are now a statutory requirement and there is a service in every LEA. Services are supported by unparalleled levels of funding. However, this funding now comes through the LEA's core budget, not as a separately defined funding stream. The level of correspondence between the Council and LEAs over the new funding arrangements shows that many LEAs were not aware of these changes. It also suggests that there will be a continuing dialogue about the necessary level of service and the necessary level of funding in order to meet the expectations of LEAs and the minimum standards for services now set out in the Code of Practice (DfES 2001a). Services will need to be able to demonstrate how they are contributing to improved partnerships between parents and schools and parents and the LEA. In addition, services will increasingly be asked to demonstrate how they are contributing to the main LEA agenda of school improvement and pupil progress.

Another consequence of permanent Parent Partnership Services is that those who manage them and staff them will have reasonable expectations of opportunities for professional development. However, even taken together nationally, Parent Partnership Coordinators constitute a very small group, and a group from a variety of professional backgrounds. Links have been established between the Council and a range of national, regional and local bodies who provide education and training. These links need to be developed further if the Council is to support services in accessing wider opportunities for professional development.

A concern for more consistent standards has also led to an initiative, funded by the DfES, to develop a national training package for Independent Parental Supporters. The Council is providing the support for this work, but importantly it is a collaborative piece of work between the LEA-funded services and voluntary agencies. It is likely that national expectations and developments in the Network will increasingly call for collaborative approaches of this sort.

It is likely that support for the Network will increasingly involve the Council in a dialogue with LEAs as well as services. Part of the dialogue with LEAs may continue to be about the effective use of their Parent Partnership resources. Such discussions are likely to require more detailed comparative information than has been available to date. It is likely that the development of collaborative work between NPPN, **napps**, LEAs, the SEN Regional Partnerships and the DfES would best serve this need. Work in this area could sensibly connect with the DfES' work on a national framework for accountability.

The development of the work on standards in the Practice Guide will be an important way for services to articulate for themselves more of the detail of the work in supporting parents and something of the balance to be struck in the work. As a finite resource services already find themselves stretched across a number of demands. There are tensions between:

- providing the individual support for parents and developing a culture of partnership across schools and the LEA;
- the proper management of services by LEAs and the provision of independent advice;
- the statutory requirement for a service and the impact of funding changes;
- the need to develop partnerships with a range of agencies, the requirement to publicise services and the need to develop access for all.

In response to these many demands, LEAs and services will need clear priorities and plans for the development of their service to meet those priorities. Along the way, explicit standards, quality assurance measures and comparisons with services in other LEAs will play an important part in supporting the arguments for the development of Parent Partnership both locally and nationally.

References

Berridge, D. and Russell, P. (1988) *A Red Bus Next Year?* London: Haringey Local Education Authority.

Council for Disabled Children (1996) *End of Year Report to the Department for Education and Employment.* London: Council for Disabled Children.

Department for Education (1994) *Code of Practice on the Identification and Assessment of Special Educational Needs.* London: Central Office of Information.

Department for Education and Employment (1997) *Excellence for All Children: Meeting Special Educational Needs.* London: DfEE.

Department for Education and Employment (1998) *Meeting Special Educational Needs: a Programme of Action.* London: DfEE.

Department for Education and Skills (2001a) *Code of Practice on the Identification and Assessment of Special Educational Needs.* London: Department for Education and Skills.

Department for Education and Skills (2001b) *SEN Toolkit*. London: Department for Education and Skills.

GLAD (1988) *A Joint Endeavour? The Role of Parents, Parents' Groups and Voluntary Organisations in the Assessment Procedure for Special Educational Needs, in Three London Boroughs*. London: Greater London Association for the Disabled.

Henderson, E. (1998) 'A parent's views on special educational needs and the Green Paper', in National Parent Partnership Network *Newsletter*, Issue 7, March 1998, Council for Disabled Children.

House of Commons (1987) *Third Report from the Education, Science and Arts Committee, 1986–87, Special Educational Needs: Implementation of the Education Act 1981*. London: Her Majesty's Stationery Office.

Hunt, A. and Magee, W. (1998) 'Is there life after LEA funding?', in National Parent Partnership Network *Newsletter*, Issue 7, March 1998, Council for Disabled Children.

National Deaf Children's Society (1999) *Quality Standards in Education – England*. London: National Deaf Children's Society.

National Parent Partnership Newsletter (NPPN) (1995) London: CDC, October.

Russell, P. (1983) *The Role of the Named Person*. London: Voluntary Council for Handicapped Children.

Wolfendale, S. and Cook, G. (1997) *Evaluation of Parent Partnership Schemes*. Research Report No. 34. London: DfEE.

Chapter 4

Practitioners pioneering partnership: the development of napps

Dave Reid and Chris Goodwin-King

This chapter provides a background to the development of individual Parent Partnership Services, to the formation of the National Association of Parent Partnership Services (**napps**), its current role, function and aims for the future.

What will be your lasting memory of the early 1990s? The adventures of Wallace and Grommit or the Teenage Mutant Hero Turtles? The virtual reality of Tamagotchi and Sonic the Hedgehog? The construction of the Channel Tunnel or screening of *Schindler's List*? During 1994 the introduction of the National Lottery created a few millionaires, but of benefit to many was the publication of *The Code of Practice on the Identification and Assessment of Special Educational Needs* (DfEE 1994).

The Code also created a new breed of individual, namely, 'Parent Partnership Officer/Coordinator/Worker'. In the early days of the Code the predominant titles for those working in Parent Partnership was Officer or sometimes Coordinator. The majority of authorities have now adopted the term coordinator for newly created posts in line with the description of the post in the revised Code of Practice.

Early beginnings

In Hampshire, a Parent Partnership Scheme was introduced on 1 June 1994 with little more than a copy of the Code of Practice and a desk – and with the challenge to create something from nothing. On the assumption that there would be other schemes experiencing similar beginnings, Hampshire contacted over 40 other local education authorities on 20 June 1994 to enquire if they had established a Parent Partnership Scheme yet, and to propose the introduction of networking between Parent Partnership practitioners to facilitate support and share information/experiences. The response was very positive and resulted in an inaugural network meeting taking place in Winchester on 17 August 1994, attended by representatives from 27

Parent Partnership Schemes. There was a formal programme for the day combining presentations from Philippa Russell (Council for Disabled Children) and Caroline Hemson (Advisory Centre for Education), with group work on the role of the Named Person and topics relevant to the work of schemes nationwide. The issues raised through discussion can be summarised as follows:

- Could parents opt *not* to have a Named Person? If so, would the LEA still have a responsibility to notify parents of Named Person contact?
- Would it be advisable to introduce parents to the role of the Named Person when their child is at Stage 2 of the school-based assessment (or even Stage 1), and to ensure teachers' awareness of the Named Person role?
- Would it be good practice to inform parents of Named Person contact in the letter they receive initiating formal assessment?
- Who would have responsibility for screening Named Persons – police checks, etc.?
- Should local education authorities develop and deliver training packages for Named Persons?
- Could a school governor responsible for SEN, in one school, act as a Named Person for parents of a child in another?
- Could there be a difference between someone who parents could trust as a Named Person and someone who can offer them advice about their child's special educational needs?
- Would a set of guidelines for Named Persons be helpful, covering person specification, role parameters, training/support, task specification, etc., to assist parents in making a realistic choice of Named Person, i.e. someone who can support/represent them in an effective, objective way?
- How would Named Person 'turnover' be managed?
- Should a Named Person be an individual or organisation?
- If a parent has not nominated a Named Person at the draft state-ment stage, should there be penalties/comebacks if the LEA failed to inform parents of a Named Person contact?
- If the LEA were responsible for recommending the name of a Named Person to parents at draft statement stage, how indepen-dent would that Named Person be?
- How would expenses incurred by Named Persons be covered? If the LEA were to reimburse expenses, how independent would the Named Person be?
- If the LEA, via the Parent Partnership Coordinator/Officer, was responsible for identifying, training and supporting Named Persons, how could they be independent from the LEA? Would such a system be manageable, i.e. similar to LEA running its own

volunteer bureau? Would there be a practical alternative, i.e. voluntary groups' identifying/supporting Named Persons?

- Who would be responsible for insurance for Named Persons?
- How could an 'ideal' match of Named Persons to parents be achieved, when a variety of individuals' needs and personalities have to be taken into account? How would the matching process be managed?

If any of this sounds familiar in the context of today's work, it may well be supposed that the 'Named Person' has just been changed to 'Independent Parental Supporter', and Parent Partnership has not moved on at all? Is any of this still relevant today? Where services have chosen to work with a volunteer group of workers, some of the above will be recognisable and current. However, what is important to bear in mind is the ruminations cited were the *only* discussions taking place at the inception of Parent Partnership Services. Agendas at regional meetings and national liaison group discussions today bear witness to the development and growth of a service still developing and growing but certainly more mature and 'professional' in every sense of the word.

The following key issues were identified during this first conference:

- The strength of LEA relationship with voluntary agencies/groups.
- The extent of authority a Parent Partnership Coordinator/Officer has to initiate/influence change.
- The level of knowledge of a Parent Partnership Coordinator/ Officer on broader issues, e.g. transport policy.
- The importance of gaining access to key people with regard to decision-making and information channels.
- The need for a Parent Partnership Coordinator/Officer to have knowledge and understanding of how special educational provision in schools is resourced.
- Would it be the responsibility of a Parent Partnership Coordinator/Officer to ensure that information provided through LEA to parents is both accurate and appropriate?
- Concern over the temporary nature of Parent Partnership posts.
- The need for Parent Partnership Coordinator/Officers to be aware of their LEA's training policy and current methods of delivery to avoid duplication of activity.
- A key aspect of the role would be influencing changes in attitudes towards working in partnership with parents, e.g. influencing schools to use enterprise in the way they involve/ inform parents.
- The need for a clear definition of the role of the Parent Partnership Coordinator/Officer.

- The requirement for a mechanism to evaluate the needs of parents and evidence that such needs are being addressed/met, such as workshops, questionnaires, informal meetings, etc.
- The importance of evaluating school policies in relation to home–school contact and in seeking the views of parents.
- The clarity of the relationship between Parent Partnership coordinator/officer and schools, influencing the quality and nature of the relationship between schools and parents, involvement of Parent Partnership function with teacher training/INSET.
- The evolving role of the Parent Partnership coordinator/officer over time and the need for development plans to reflect changing needs and demands.
- The importance of specifying *realistic* performance indicators for the Parent Partnership Scheme, and the need for a measure of the outcomes. The consensus view was that a reduction in number of appeals was an unrealistic performance indicator.
- The importance of focusing, after September 1994 and the introduction of the Code of Practice, on the future in a fresh and positive light and not carrying forward any dissatisfaction resulting from 'old' regulations.
- The concept of the Parent Partnership Scheme being a source of information (not advice) for parents.

Thus, **napps** suggests that practitioners should still continue to ask searching and relevant questions of colleagues within their authorities but now is the time for solutions to be found and offered from within our own practice, rather than waiting for someone outside our service to decide on direction and funding. The issue of funding is crucial to the successful development of services, in allowing response to the needs not only of parents but also professionals facing issues on working with parents. As practitioners we must ensure that we have a broader role and take responsibility to create the right climate for our own successful practice.

That early meeting provided a springboard for the introduction of a number of regional networks including one in the south-east, which held its first meeting in November 1994 – again in Winchester. Subsequent meetings took place termly at venues throughout the south-east region – from Hampshire in the west to Kent in the east.

During the period 1995–97 Parent Partnership Schemes evolved according to local conditions and priorities, which resulted in a diversity of structure, resource and function on both a regional and national basis. There was evidence through the networks to confirm that, despite diversity, there was consistency in the contribution which schemes were making to:

- impartiality;
- influencing the decision-making process within LEAs;
- improving partnership between all stakeholders: parents, young people, voluntary and statutory agencies;
- strengthening the role of parents in decision-making and contributing to the development of Parent Partnership Schemes and LEA provision;
- developing the range, quality and sources of information available for parents.

However, there was still uncertainty about whether Parent Partnership Schemes were here to stay. At the time many were still operating on annual contracts with no guarantee of future funding; functioning with limited staffing levels and feeling isolation – not being regarded as 'core' provision by their respective LEAs. Even the term 'scheme' could be viewed in the mindset of some as meaning temporary provision. The widely adopted term 'service' suggests a sustainable resource.

The next phase

From the very beginning Parent Partnership Schemes had been resourced through funding available from the Department for Education, known as Grants for Education Support and Training (GEST). Individual services were required to submit annual bids to the DfES (the current name) to access this resource during the period 1995–97. However, this funding was to be discontinued in 1997, threatening the very existence of some services. Sadly a few were disbanded during 1997 whereas others were sustained either through core funding within LEAs or alternative sources of grant aid.

In the Eastern Region at this time only three of the ten LEAs continued in any substantive way with Parent Partnership Services. When Hertfordshire appointed a Parent Partnership coordinator in 1994 on a permanent contract, it was believed to be the only LEA in England at that time to do so. Suffolk converted a fixed-term contract to a permanent contract because of established successful practice. Bedfordshire also retained their Parent Partnership Officer throughout this time of change but only Hertfordshire and Suffolk continued to meet on a regular and cooperative basis. During this period of post-GEST funding, other Parent Partnership Services continued to meet. For practical purposes this was generally with geographical neighbours.

Within the south-east Parent Partnership network there was discussion as to how Parent Partnership work could achieve greater recognition and status on a national basis. Acknowledging the valuable contribution being made by the National Parent Partnership

Network (NPPN) to the profile of our work, would it now be appropriate for Parent Partnership practitioners to take responsibility for developing a national identity, both for political and professional purposes?

The South-East region distributed a survey questionnaire in January 1997 seeking opinions on two options:

1. forming a national association managed by Parent Partnership practitioners themselves;
2. aligning Parent Partnership with an existing professional body.

Thirty-five services responded to the survey, of which 51 per cent favoured option (1) and 31 per cent favoured both options. The results clearly endorsed the development of a professional body.

Launching the National Association of Parent Partnership Services

The National Association of Parent Partnership Services or **napps** was originally set up to raise awareness of Parent Partnership Services and the work they were undertaking across England and Wales. Parent Partnership coordinators/officers historically worked in relative isolation within their own authorities leading to the development of a great diversity of services, responsibilities and resources. This all offered a wealth of ideas to exchange, with *ad hoc* regional networks starting to grow in membership but again there was no strategic approach to national policy or practice. All this was happening a long time before the NPPN considered writing a Practice Guide or the DfES considered creating anything with 'Parent Partnership Good Practice' in the title. However, we did have a research report to refer to. The work, carried out, on behalf of the DfEE, by Wolfendale and Cook, entitled *Evaluation of Special Educational Needs Parent Partnership Schemes* (1997), listed the elements of an effective Parent Partnership Service.

In July 1997 the South-East region contacted other Parent Partnership regional networks to seek representation for a working group to explore the feasibility of establishing a professional association. Total commitment was given and representatives from each region had initial meetings in London in November 1997 and March 1998. Eight practitioners, representing regional networks from England and Wales, shared their concerns and attempted to explore common practice within the regional networks. These representatives endorsed the idea of forming a national liaison group which had a common purpose rooted in policy and practice. The sense of ownership is crucial in informing the professional role of Parent

Partnership practitioners. A mission statement was agreed at the **napps** Liaison Group meeting and sent out for consultation to the eight regional networks. The following gained national approval and was subsequently adopted.

The National Association of Parent Partnership Services (**napps**) promotes effective Parent Partnership within education, recognising the diversity of services available nationally. The aims of the Association will be pursued through close liaison with the National Parent Partnership Network, NASEN and other interested organisations. **napps** aims to do the following:

- define professional standards and quality of service;
- develop good practice;
- enhance and expand on the work of existing Parent Partnership networks;
- inform and influence policy – locally and nationally;
- promote collaboration between regional networks;
- encourage new initiatives;
- promote cost-effective purchase of resources;
- work closely with other national organisations such as the National Parent Partnership Network (NPPN) and the National Association of Special Educational Needs (NASEN).

It was agreed to meet three times a year, in London, and set up a regular link at these meetings with the DfES and NPPN. Each individual Parent Partnership Service is a member of **napps**. In turn, they have the opportunity to attend regional networks meetings and finally the regional networks have a voice through their representative on the national liaison group (see Figure 4.1).

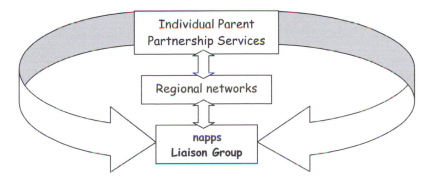

Figure 4.1 Parent Partnership network

A weekend away

To launch **napps** the liaison group planned a residential weekend at a hotel in Hinckley, Leicestershire in November 1999. Delegates representing organisations involved in all aspects of Parent Partnership were present. The weekend was organised in conjunction with a NASEN conference, which provided financial support and administrative expertise for planning and delivery of the event. This joint planning venture worked well and would be worth revisiting in the future where Parent Partnership Services wished to hold an event but need professional advice and practical support.

Although the context of the three-day conference was Parent Partnership, the liaison group took the opportunity to officially launch **napps** after dinner on Saturday evening. Both the vice-chair and chair of the group encouraged delegates to participate in regional networks and liaise on both a formal and an informal basis.

All those who provide a Parent Partnership Service are welcome to join a regional network and thus are represented at national level. At present there are no costs involved apart from local arrangements within regional networks and minor financial arrangements made in order that liaison group members are able to attend meetings three times a year in London. These arrangements are supported by a small grant from the DfES. The grant, given for the first time in 2001, demonstrates that **napps** is being taken seriously as representative of an important national network of services. It is valued as a consultative body offering the voice of practitioners throughout England and Wales. This is demonstrated by **napps** being consulted on the revisions to the Code of Practice in early 2001.

Each regional group has the opportunity to have a representative on the national liaison group. The Parent Partnership regions are Eastern, East Midlands, West Midlands, London, North East, Yorkshire and Humberside, North West, South East and Central, South West and Wales.[1]

The national liaison group represents both statutory and voluntary sector post holders reflecting the diversity of those providing the Parent Partnership Service on behalf of each local authority. All Parent Partnership Coordinators/Officers would benefit from making links with their regional group.

A representative for the Special Needs Division at the DfES has a standing agenda item at **napps** meetings each term to provide up-to-date information about national initiatives from the DfES. This has been particularly important as the Code of Practice has progressed

---

[1]For more information contact Chris Goodwin-King on 01992 555922 or write to her at Parent Partnership, Children, Schools and Families, Hertfordshire County Council, County Hall, Hertford SG13 8DF.

through its various revisions and the liaison group was heavily involved with the consultation on Chapter 2 'Working in Partnership with Parents'.

A representative from NPPN also has a standing agenda item at our meetings to provide up-to-date information about national initiatives and opportunities for collaborative working with the Council for Disabled Children and the National Parent Partnership Network in particular (see Chapter 3). Initiatives such as the Practice Guide will be taken forward nationally and the Eastern Region Parent Partnership Group has been working on this project with NPPN for more than a year.

The regional aspect of Parent Partnership has now been given increased emphasis as all DfES Regional Partnerships have the role of Parent Partnership Service on their agenda. Details of Regional Partnerships can be found on the DfES website. The networks of Parent Partnership Services and DfES Regional Partnerships are not always co-terminous. While this does not matter at some levels, the Regional Partnership Coordinator is also creating diverse links with senior officers and services beyond education, for example, he or she can become a useful catalyst for two-way information exchange at regional Parent Partnership Services meetings. This creates an opportunity for a positive and effective promotion of our work. In the Eastern Region Parent Partnership Services are represented on the DfES Partnership Steering Group.

The association is an effective method of sharing ideas and disseminating information at a national level and depends upon input from its members. Regional representatives should be kept up to date with issues that need to be raised at the national forum and the national group will provide feedback to regions on issues raised regionally at liaison group meetings. In this respect the timing of meetings at all levels is important. Each regional group is not only represented on the **napps** liaison group but also on the NPPN steering group and working groups. Meetings need to be arranged to ensure that agendas interact and there is continuous flow throughout the **napps** structure.

Benchmarking

Currently **napps** is carrying out a benchmarking activity across England and Wales. Two things prompted this development:

1. Best Value reviews of local authority services.
2. Evaluation of some Parent Partnership posts which have resulted in a downgrading of salary.

Exercises such as this flow quite easily from the liaison group, in the same way that a pebble creates ripples when it is thrown into a pool. The eight representatives create the task, informed and prompted by individual services needs. The task is then undertaken within the regional networks and responses are fed back to the liaison group who collate the findings. These are then fed back to the individual services who can then use the data for their own purposes within their own authority, e.g. to provide evidence to seek to influence decision-makers.

The benefit of networking in this way is that Parent Partnership Services are recognised as belonging to a national network. The association has a strategic view of the work across England and Wales and can provide support and influence, particularly where services are small and/or offered on a part-time basis.

As the current allocations of Standards Fund end in March 2002, Parent Partnership Services are in a far stronger position than they were at the end of GEST funding in 1997. Not only because they now have statutory status but also because more practitioners are employed on permanent contracts, and many services are teams rather than individuals. Many Parent Partnership Coordinators/ Officers are well-paid senior managers within local authorities. These colleagues are best able to influence policy and practice and offer strategic insight into the authority's work with parents, across a broad range of inclusive activities. Where Parent Partnership Services have not been established in this way, the data collected by **napps** can help to influence new thinking at this time of change in funding arrangements and in the context of the revised Code of Practice. The revised Code devotes Chapter 2 to the issues of a range of professional considerations when working with parents.

The future

As successful practitioners we now have confidence in **napps** to think ahead to future developments for the association. It may be possible for a post to be created to service the needs of the association should funding for NPPN cease. The post would act in a coordinating role, drawing together all the strands of the individual services and regional networks. Currently this does not happen as the association is made up of practitioner members, some of who perform the role within the authority on a part-time basis with no administrative support. It is not feasible or desirable that any members are taken off task to try and service the needs of the association, and at present this is a valuable function that NPPN perform. The regional groups and the liaison group are able to service themselves from their own resources.

The NPPN ICT (Information and Communications Technology) forum, created by BECTa (British Educational Communications and Technology Agency), is a useful development in linking individuals with other services and colleagues they would not meet regionally. Clearly there are still developmental issues associated with this site which need to be resolved but essentially it is a self-supporting method of interaction.

napps has now made contact with national organisations, both statutory and voluntary, for the purpose of mutual information exchange and consultation. These organisations include the Disability Rights Commission, Home Office, National Association for Gifted Children, and the main political parties.

Effective communication networks have been established and **napps** needs to continue as a consultative body of practitioners. It also needs to raise issues within current and future national agendas. Parent Partnership Services have taken great strides since 1994 to develop a supportive and innovative professional group. Anyone attending a meeting of Parent Partnership practitioners recently will have observed that issues and discussions are wide-ranging and thought-provoking, demonstrating the swift development of a relatively embryonic service. All practitioners should be proud of where their service has come from and be excited by the journey ahead.

References

DfEE (1994) *Code of Practice on the Identification and Assessment of Special Educational Needs.* London: DfEE.

Wolfendale, S. and Cook. G. (1997) *Evaluation of Special Educational Needs Parent Partnership Schemes.* Research Report No. 34. London: DfEE.

Part 2

Illustrations from Practice in Parent Partnership Services

Chapter 5

Parent Partnership and school improvement: an Eastern Region perspective

Eithne Leming

Introduction

This chapter describes the development of the Eastern Region Parent Partnership group and the particular model adopted by the Suffolk Parent Partnership Service. The contribution that the Parent Partnership Service has made in Suffolk to the mainstream education agenda of school improvement is described and used to illustrate the distinctive aspects of this model, which are characterised by its 'inclusive' and strategic approach.

Context

Suffolk is a large rural county, which forms part of the Eastern Region group of local authorities. The Eastern Region has a strong tradition of working together wherever possible to maximise resources, share expertise and build on each other's experiences. It comprises ten LEAs, four unitary ones and six large ones, mainly in rural counties.

The Suffolk Parent Partnership Service was established in September 1994 with the help of monies from DfEE Grants for Education Support and Training (GEST). At the same time (September 1994) the Eastern Region Group of Parent Partnership Services was established.

In March 1997 when the GEST funding came to an end there were only two members of the Eastern Region group remaining: Suffolk and Hertfordshire. The group was always both active and productive and attempted to work strategically. Collaborative ventures included the organisation of a National Conference, a workshop for members of the Society for Education Officers, production of posters and leaflets for schools and the start of a benchmarking exercise. Then, in April 1998, the appointment of an SEN Regional Project Coordinator further assisted this process when the Parent Partnership work became part of the remit of the project.

In geographical terms, Suffolk, along with some of the other Eastern Region counties, is an area of contrasts, ranging from affluent market towns to urban areas with levels of poverty, which qualify for EU funding. Even in some of the more rural parts of the county, alongside apparent affluence among some of the farming communities, poverty exists and a lack of basic services such as public transport can further compound the problem. The existence of military bases also brings the challenges of a transient population.

There are 350 schools in Suffolk serving a compulsory school-age population of approximately 100,000. There are 3,300 pupils with Statements of SEN, a large proportion of whom are catered for within mainstream settings. There are currently eight Special Schools and seven Pupil Referral Units.

The Suffolk Parent Partnership Model

In Suffolk the service was based centrally within the LEA in the section responsible for policy development across the county and across services. Initially, due to the conditions of the funding, the focus was on parents of children with special educational needs. However, when the GEST funding came to an end in March 1997, the focus of the permanently funded Parent Partnership post was broadened beyond SEN.

The purpose of the new post was to work strategically to assist the LEA and schools to develop effective partnerships with parents. The aims of the service are to support local parents in order to raise pupil achievement by doing the following:

- identifying the information and support needs of parents and carers through consultation and research;
- providing information and developing practical and positive services to suit their needs;
- helping schools, Education Department staff and parents to work in partnership through the provision of training.

The Parent Partnership Service aims to be an inclusive one. It provides discrete services for parents of pupils with SEN, such as a helpline and a range of courses for parents, all developed on the basis of data collected from parents using a range of systematic research and consultation methodologies. The courses offered have been designed for various groups of parents who are at particular risk of social exclusion such as:

- parents of children with special needs;
- parents of children with long-term medical needs that prevent regular school attendance; and
- parents of children with emotional and behavioural needs.

This group-based support is designed to do the following:

- to help parents identify their own information and support needs, in order that their children's needs can be met more effectively;
- to enable parents to develop skills and build confidence in communicating with their children and with professionals who work with their children, and in particular, to develop negotiation and assertion skills;
- to help parents develop their own support networks and thereby reduce a sense of isolation.

The service firmly rejects the deficit view of parents based on assumptions that parents will automatically need specialised support on an ongoing individualised basis to help them negotiate with professionals. The group work and individual service offered via the helpline do not offer advice or guidance. Instead these services enable parents, through the provision of impartial information appropriate to their needs and listening, which is both active and reflective, to identify their options and make their own choices.

Access to services is open. There are no eligibility criteria determining access to services. Staff from statutory and voluntary agencies provide information about services but do not act as gatekeepers, deciding who should have access. Instead, parents self-refer based on their view that the service is suitable for them.

Although based within the local authority, the Suffolk Parent Partnership Service has a development group, which includes staff from schools, other statutory and voluntary agencies and is chaired by a parent. The purpose of the group, as the name suggests, is to help develop partnership working between parents and staff from a range of agencies.

The development plan for the service is based on the results of tri-annual stakeholder surveys involving a range of parents (many of whom do not have children with SEN), staff from schools, the LEA and voluntary agencies. Information is provided, as part of the survey, on progress and data collected from service user evaluations. Respondents are asked to help set priorities for the future.

The first of these surveys (carried out in March 1996), identified work with schools as the greatest priority, particularly raising awareness of parental issues and development of skills to assist communication between parents and school staff. The second, which took place in March 1999, again identified work with schools as a major priority and work with groups of parents who may be more difficult to reach and to involve in the education of their children.

In summary, the key characteristics of the Suffolk Parent Partnership model are the following:

- it is strategic, using existing organisational structures as well as current local and national agendas, as conduits to facilitate changes in culture and practice from within;
- it seeks to encourage inclusion through systems and practices that celebrate diversity and enable people to participate in mainstream activities rather than ones that create dependency or that view difference as a deficit requiring compensatory support or treatment;
- it works from a community development base, using consultation and research, identifying needs and views of parents, pupils, voluntary organisations, school and LEA staff;
- it develops new services and reviews current services to meet the needs identified.

Figure 5.1 shows the network of services.

Figure 5.1

> Steady under the strain and strong through tension,
> Its feet on both sides but in neither camp,
> It stands its ground, a span of pure attention,
> A holding action, the arches and the ramp
> Steady under strain and strong through tension.
>
> (Seamus Heaney 2001)

The model has foundations firmly based in the community, developing services based on the needs of users, such as parents, pupils and schools. The strategic planning role of the local authority assists in the delivery of services using the expertise of both the voluntary and statutory agencies in multidisciplinary approaches. As the poem suggests, with feet based on either side, but in neither camp, the model gains strength from the tension of the spanning action.

The impact of parent partnership on school improvement

From the early days work with schools was a priority. Indeed, two pieces of research into the work of Parent Partnership Services raised the importance of this strand of the work. The first was Wolfendale and Cook (1997) and more recently Vernon (1999). Changes in the relationships between schools and LEAs, such as local management of schools and fair funding arrangements, have meant that schools have become much more autonomous and the role of the LEA has become much more 'light touch' and distant, even where services such as those for pupils with Statements of SEN funded by the LEA are delivered on a day-to-day basis by schools. As the providers, schools are, therefore, in much more direct and constant contact with parents than the LEA.

The work of the Suffolk Parent Partnership Service has a very high profile within the local authority. Recently Suffolk LEA was awarded Beacon Status for its work on school improvement and one of the reasons given for its success in gaining this award was the Parent Partnership work aimed at improving home–school links using a variety of strategies, including preventative mediation services. In addition, Suffolk County Council won the Council of the Year Award in March 2001 and the Parent Partnership Service contributed by presenting some of its work to the judges. Aspects of Parent Partnership Service work were provided as evidence to illustrate the success of the Access and Community Involvement Panel which forms part of the new political structures of the local authority.

Examples of school improvement work

School pyramid-based community projects

The development of school pyramid-based community projects illustrates several of the distinctive strands of the work. These projects serve groups or pyramids of schools and have been sited in areas which receive a high rating on the county's index of multiple deprivation. These projects offer an outreach service that is designed to be inclusive in the sense that it aims to reach parents and carers who are either suffering or who are at risk of social exclusion. Again, referrals are parent-led rather than professional-led, relying on informal parent networks and innovative outreach approaches.

The aim of the individual work with parents is to assist them to access more mainstream support services and to develop social networks. The group work which is offered as an integral part of these projects is key in helping to build self-esteem and skills to communicate more effectively with their children and the staff who work with their children. Building the skills and the confidence of parents helps to remove some of the barriers that make it difficult for them to become positively involved in their children's education; 85 per cent of parents who have used these services say that they feel more confident about talking to staff.

However, these projects strive for balance and are designed to build capacity on both sides of the bridge. For this reason, work with schools is an important and integral part of these projects. Some of the barriers that prevent effective partnership exist within the school's organisational structures and human resources in the form of staff attitudes and skills. Work with the school is therefore, twofold, offering strategic support at an organisational level and support to individual staff members through professional development opportunities designed to develop confidence and skills among both teaching and non-teaching staff.

The services for parents are completely confidential. Trust is essential on both sides. Boundaries need to be carefully established and the impartiality of the project worker is essential. Evidence collected from school staff and parents suggests that parents and staff alike value this aspect. Both the individual and group work can, with the agreement of parents, also be used as a means of collecting data in an anonymous way from parents. Such qualitative information, when organised thematically, provides valuable evidence of factors that act as inhibitors and promoters of partnership. This evidence is a valuable tool to be used as a basis for staff training and to make recommendations about organisational change that may be needed.

This kind of project work which builds capacity within schools and within the parent body can be viewed as an early form of mediation service. It assists school staff at an individual level, and particularly some parents, to feel confident enough to raise issues and negotiate solutions. It also works at an organisational level to develop openness, responsiveness and cooperation for the benefits of pupils. Quotes from two members of staff illustrates these points:

> Parental contact with the school has increased as parents realised what the school is trying to do for their child. Pupils also realised that parents, and school represented a united front with their best interests at heart.

> This work with parents has served to dramatically reinforce the home–school links thus providing a firm foundation upon which the school may place the variety of opportunities we provide. The successful outcomes of such opportunities prove to be far more positive in cases where the Parent Partnership Service has been accessed by parents.

Ofsted observed of one project:

> The school is successful in providing a variety of opportunities for parents to meet and express their opinions . . . To make it easier for parents to tackle any problems they have, and to share thoughts and ideas about their children, the school hosts a weekly confidential service called 'Choices', run by the local education authority's Parent Partnership Service.

Staff identified, through evaluations, a number of significant improvements for pupils and for the school's links with parents. Benefits for pupils noted by staff included noticeable improvements in behaviour, attendance, achievement, motivation and relationships with peers and with staff. In the area of home–school links, staff reported closer contact with parents, parents taking more initiative with communication, increased attendance at parents' meetings and support for the school's behaviour policy. Follow-up research identified that the benefits were not only sustained in all areas, but six months later further significant improvements could be noted. From the parents' perspective more than two years later they were able to report that skills learned from the service were still being used. 'I feel much more positive about myself, and I'm able to express myself with my family. It's helped me in talking to professionals – teachers, doctors, etc.'

A Pupil Referral Unit (PRU) for young children with emotional and behavioural difficulties now runs regularly, with assistance from the Parent Partnership Service, the Positive About Parenting course that was specially developed for this group of parents. A recent Ofsted report (2001) rated the work with parents as 'outstanding' and made a number of very positive comments: 'The Unit has an outstandingly successful partnership with parents. A key feature is the involvement of parents through the parenting course.'

The Unit also has an outreach service that includes work with the pupils' mainstream schools. So parents and the Unit staff also need to work closely with local schools. 'The tripartite approach, with close links between school, unit and parents gives children the best possible chance by ensuring consistency of approach, especially in behaviour management . . . The partnership is highly effective.' These comments from Ofsted endorse the views of staff and parents about the success of the work in raising pupil achievement and also illustrate the contribution to improving school effectiveness.

This approach for parents of pupils with emotional and behavioural difficulties forms an important part of Suffolk's strategy as set out in the Behaviour Support Plan, and the Parent Partnership Service has key responsibilities within part of the plan. The Positive About Parenting work with PRUs has proved so successful that following a review of Suffolk's provision for pupils with emotional and behavioural difficulties, a new and permanent post was created in April 2001 to help further develop this initiative across the county.

Policy development

An important area of work with schools has involved using parental feedback to help develop school policies. Some examples include work on home–school links, including communication and social activities organised by the Parent Teacher Association, the development of Individual Education Plans to increase accessibility for parents and pupils, and transitional planning.

Collection of data from parents has largely been through workshops or focus groups. These sessions have used informal discussion and the group process to help explore parental views about areas for investigation identified by the school in discussion with the PPO.

Sometimes staff and parent discussion groups are used to collect data. This method requires sensitive facilitation, in order that parents are not inhibited in their contributions. It has an advantage as a method because, once issues and any concerns have been aired, priorities and future actions can be planned together working from group consensus.

Data collection and dissemination

An advantage of a Parent Partnership Service established within the LEA is that it has easier access to a range of data, including data collection and dissemination routes. In Suffolk the PPO has responsibilities as a plan holder for three action plans outlining activities related to the Education Development Plan, under the heading of Engaging and Involving Parents in the Education of their Children. Two of these plans involve either the collection of data, in the form of consultation or use of this data to inform practice in schools.

Some examples of data collection include:

- research into the assessment and provision for pupils with an Autistic Spectrum Disorder, from the perspective of pupils, parents, school and LEA staff;
- a survey into the implementation of home–school agreements from the perspectives of parents, school staff and governors;
- the views of parents collected as part of parenting courses or workshops about aspects of home–school practice.

Information collected is analysed and provided in a variety of formats, for purposes of dissemination. Some examples include:

- leaflets for parents such as, *Raising Concerns, Information Schools Like to Receive from Parents*;
- guidance for school staff such as strategies for communicating and consulting with parents, design and content of home–school agreements and the views of ethnic minority parents about home–school communication;
- content for in-service training.

A book entitled *Working with Parents* (Leming 2000) has also been produced using this information. It has been designed as a self-evaluative tool for schools and includes checklists and examples of success criteria. This has been published by the Secondary Heads Association and has been disseminated nationally to its membership. Dissemination through professional networks has proved to be particularly effective in influencing practice in schools.

All Ofsted reports of Suffolk Schools are also analysed. The data collected from parents as part of the Inspection's parental question-naire survey and parents' meetings are collated as well as the judge-ments made by Inspectors of the school's work with parents. An annual report of the findings is produced and includes analysis by school phase and type of provision. Comparisons are also made between the Inspector's judgements and the first-hand data collected from parents. Schools are encouraged to use this information as benchmarking data and the report is circulated to schools and advisers for this purpose. The most recent report has been posted on the DfES School Standards and Effectiveness website as an example of effective practice.

Guidance has been produced following the survey conducted of home–school agreements. In addition to views being sought from parents and school staff about the process of consultation, schools were also requested to provide copies of the home–school agreement produced for their school. These documents were analysed for content, format and vocabulary used. As a result of the analysis, guidance was produced providing practical advice about wording, subject areas, formats and, in particular, ways of achieving the 'balance' that was emphasised as being so important in the guidance produced by the DfES on home–school agreements.

In-service training for school staff

A number of INSET sessions are offered as part of an annual programme offered to school staff to support their work with parents.

Due to the geography of the county there are three Professional Development Centres serving the county and so each session is repeated three times. The content has been developed from research and consultation with parents and subjects include:

- day-to-day communication – written and telephone contact with parents;
- face-to-face – parent–teacher interviews;
- working with angry and distressed parents;
- delivering bad news;
- involving parents who are difficult to reach;
- receiving positive and negative feedback from parents – including complaints procedures;
- parents and teachers as co-educators.

Over the past two years 250 staff from 78 schools have attended sessions and evaluations demonstrate high levels of satisfaction. For example 99 per cent believed that the session had a positive impact on their work in school and 97 per cent felt that the content and style of the session were effective.

Sometimes these sessions are delivered as part of whole-school in-service training, especially, though not exclusively in project schools. In large high schools training may be delivered to particular groups of staff such as Heads of Year, or others with pastoral responsibilities.

There are a series of leaflets that accompany the sessions, each with a helpful checklist of good practice. These were developed with the assistance of the Parent Partnership Officer from Hertfordshire as part of a regional initiative and examples of these are provided on the DfES website page.

Some governor training has also been provided. This tends to be focused on:

- the statutory responsibilities of schools for work with parents, such as provision of information, home–school agreements, complaints procedures, and consultation;
- the more strategic aspects such as development of communication strategies and use of parental views to inform the school improvement or development plan.

In addition, as part of the LEA's package of support to governors, a folder has been produced as a self-evaluative tool for governing bodies. The Parent Partnership Service designed, with assistance from a governor, the section aimed at developing the school's work with parents.

Support to schools of concern

Support in the form of consultancy work is also provided to schools of concern including those in Special Measures. This is provided in collaboration with colleagues who are members of teams called Core Action Groups. Examples of work undertaken include project work as described above and advice about involving and communicating with parents to help gain or maintain parental confidence in the school. In some cases, advice on and involvement in collection of parent views are provided.

Involvement of the voluntary sector

Another feature of the school improvement work is the involvement of voluntary organisations to help extend and promote capacity both within the school and within the community that the school serves. Involvement of the voluntary sector also helps promote stronger links within the wider community and facilitates an exchange of skills, expertise and knowledge between voluntary and statutory organisations for the benefit of families and the organisations themselves.

Conclusion

In Suffolk the Parent Partnership Service capitalises on its position within the LEA to work strategically to assist a key function of the LEA which is its responsibilities and role in supporting school improvement. The approach is inclusive. It is based on developing practice in schools for working with the whole parental body rather than focusing only on issues for parents of children with special needs. However, within this approach some of the particular issues relating to parents of children with SEN, or other vulnerable groups such as ethnic minorities, or carers of looked-after children, are highlighted. This ensures that awareness of the needs of those groups of pupils and their parents, who are at risk of particular disadvantage, is raised within mainstream activities designed to support practice in schools.

In common with the services provided for parents, the services for schools are designed to create independence rather than dependency. Support for both parents and schools is specifically aimed at helping both client groups to identify their strengths and build on these as well as to identify their own needs and priorities for future development or action. This approach firmly rejects a deficit model; instead it helps each to take responsibility for finding solutions from within and to enable rather than encourage helplessness or dependency.

The promotion of this kind of self-advocacy is distinctly different from the more usual form of advocacy where a third party acts as the voice, speaking on behalf of another. The Suffolk model is based on the belief that self-advocacy facilitates partnership. Like the bridge described in the poem quoted above, 'Its feet on both sides, but in neither camp . . . It stands its ground, a span of pure attention, A holding action.' By promoting self-advocacy there is an impartiality which performs a holding action so that partners can tread their own path across the bridge towards the other side. The balance is a difficult one requiring support to both parties that recognises the different needs of each. Strength is gained from strong links forged with all sections of the community and in this way the service can remain, 'Steady under the strain and strong through tension.'

In Suffolk the impact of the work of the Parent Partnership Service is demonstrated by the high profile of the work gained both nationally and locally. For example, collaborative work with the Secondary Heads Association on the development of their policy for educational inclusion and their model for the School of the Future illustrate the effective links forged with professional networks. In addition, references have been made to the Suffolk model by several DfEE research projects highlighting various aspects of Parent Partnership practice, such as the work with schools (Vernon 1999) and dispute resolution (Hall 1999). Locally, the impact can be identified at all levels from the political to the individual service user perspective. For example, the Beacon Status award for School Improvement work, our contribution to the Council of the Year Award and the positive evaluations of our service received from the voluntary sector, parents, school and LEA staff as part of our quality assurance systems indicate the impact of the service locally.

Future work must look beyond the narrow boundaries set by the early focus on parents of pupils with SEN. The distinctive issues that these parents face are best highlighted through awareness raising generally about the importance of involving parents and carers in the education of their children. While it is important that the SEN and Disability Act 2001 and the revised SEN Code of Practice establish Parent Partnership Services as an essential element of SEN services, it is also vital that the work is viewed within a wider context. Ofsted's guidance for Inspectors entitled *Evaluating Educational Inclusion* (2001) may well prove helpful in placing a greater emphasis on the importance of consulting with and involving all parents and pupils, particularly those who may be at risk of social exclusion or subject to discriminatory practice. An 'inclusive' approach to Parent Partnership, described in this chapter, has a universality, which can place it at the centre of the debate on the development of an education system fit for the twenty-first century.

References

Hall, J. (1999) *Resolving Disputes between Parents, Schools and LEAs: Some Examples of Best Practice*. London: DfES.

Heaney, S. (2001) *Electric Light*. London: Faber and Faber.

Leming, E. (2000) *Working with Parents*. Leicester: SHA.

Ofsted (2001) *Evaluating Educational Inclusion: Guidance for Inspectors and Schools*. Reference number HMI235, only available online from Ofsted Website: http://www.ofsted.gov.uk

Vernon, J. (1999) *Parent Partnership and Special Educational Needs: Perspectives on Good Practice*. Research Report No. 162. London: DfES.

Wolfendale, S. and Cook, G. (1997) *Evaluation of Special Educational Needs Parent Partnership Schemes*. Research Report No. 34. London: DfES.

Chapter 6

Parent Partnership in Walsall

Angela Jackman

Introduction

This chapter explores the development of the Parent Partnership Service in Walsall identifying gaps in provision, examining how these were addressed and assessing the effectiveness of those which worked. Areas covered include a brief history of the service, especially in the regional context, discussion of the core activities of Parent Partnership as defined by the DfES, a description of Parent Partnership's contribution to Transition Planning, service involvement in inclusion, conflict resolution and service management.

History

In 1993 the Department for Education (DFE) invited Local Education Authorities (LEAs) to apply for three-year GEST funding to establish Special Educational Needs (SEN) Parent Partnership Schemes (PPS). In common with the majority of LEAs, Walsall established a scheme. This employed one full-time officer who worked closely with the Senior Inspector for SEN. A link was formed between the LEA scheme and a local National Children's Homes (NCH) project which was extensively developed until the present situation whereby we work in partnership. Throughout the West Midlands there has consistently been a balance between LEA-managed and private sector schemes. Solihull, Dudley and Telford and Wrekin/Shropshire are entirely voluntary sector and Walsall has its link with NCH.

Walsall has always been involved in regional developments, mainly through the West Midlands branch of the National Parent Partnership Network. The support of the national network has been greatly valued in the region, particularly when the initial three-year funding for Parent Partnership Schemes came to a halt in 1997. At this time the established good practice of the majority of the schemes came to end as many LEAs either dropped the schemes altogether or drastically modified them. Birmingham had no PPS from 1996 and the majority of West Midlands schemes were reduced to part-time provision, frequently attached to statutory work. In Walsall the full-time PPO left and was replaced by the present post-holder on a permanent contract with a split post: four days per week equivalent Post-14 Transition Officer and one day per week equivalent Parent Partnership Officer.

Consultation and inter-agency collaboration

In Autumn 1996 the LEA Commission on Special Education was established which subsequently reported its findings. One area of concern was the perceived lack of parental information or support from the LEA. Parents were often unaware of procedures or available provision and they were left feeling that there was nowhere to go for support. There was also concern at a perceived lack of urgency on the part of schools and the LEA in response to requests for help from parents and regarding the quality and quantity of information passed on to them. Parents felt that there were no clearly identified channels of communication they could use to discuss their children's progress and the stage they had reached in the SEN procedures. The recommendations of the report, some of which reflect those of the revised Code of Practice, are that ways be found to do the following:

- increase inter-agency collaboration;
- review and establish policies to articulate more clearly vision philosophies for special education within the borough;
- improve liaison with parents and develop a package to provide more detailed information;
- formalise procedures and mechanisms to improve communication between the different sections of the Education Department to provide a more consistent and coordinated response;
- establish a joint database to identify casework and agency involvement;
- debate and consider the establishment of a Children's Services Sub-committee;
- continually review the range of provision to ensure that the response to the needs being identified is appropriate;
- continue to strengthen and improve the advice offered to schools regarding the establishment and reviewing of criteria for different stages of identification and assessment of SEN.

The Special Needs section of the LEA was reorganised and on the Parent Partnership front in particular several initiatives were introduced. A Parent Information Pack was produced and distributed to all parents of children with special needs at Stage 4 with the letter informing them that their child is being considered for formal assessment. The pack drew attention to the existence of the Parent Partnership Officer and gave contact details.

The extensive home visit work of the Parent Partnership Officer (PPO) when she originally took up her post was reduced by over 80 per cent.

The PPO established links with local voluntary organisations and support groups. She attends at least one group/organisation meeting per month. Groups include the local dyslexia support organisation, clubs for the visually impaired, the support group for Attention Deficit Disorder, the Parents at Work Network, etc. In her capacity as a member of the Working Group for People with a Disability she helped to establish the local Access Group (for people with disabilities and/or their carers).

In November 1997 the PPO conducted a survey of over 400 parents in response to the government's Green Paper *Excellence for All Children: Meeting Special Educational Needs* (DfEE 1997). There were 358 responses. The main findings were:

- that parents wanted more help at the school-based stages of assessment;
- that they would like more direct contact (face-to-face meetings) with schools;
- that their views should be given more credibility during the assessment process.

Overall, parents were happy with the support they received from the LEA. A number of parents made specific comments on the forms, most regarding the notion of the Named Person (there was polarisation for/against) and the suggestion that voluntary special needs organisations could help with the assessment process (again polarisation: parents of pupils in special schools were generally in favour, those of Statemented children in mainstream school against).

The PPO and inter-agency colleagues have made presentations on transition for young people with SEN, including two for the King's Fund. She also helped to organise the 1999 NASEN national conference at which she ran a transition workshop. The PPO role involves a considerable commitment to inter-agency collaboration. In Walsall the PPO represents Education on several groups contributing to the Children's Services Development Plan.

Each year the Children with a Disability Steering Group organises a consultative event for parents and young people in the special needs arena. The outcomes of these are published and circulated widely and they are used in reviewing the Children's Services Plan.

Post-14 transition planning

The PPO/Transition Officer was appointed to set up and administer the transition process for children with a Statement of Special Educational Needs. There was no consistency in the way the process was organised and implemented within the borough, and certainly not for those pupils placed in out-of-borough schools.

The Transition Officer's first task was to audit existing reviews and to write up some of them as formal Post-14 Transition Plans which fulfilled the criteria of the Code of Practice. Meetings were held with the LEA Statements Officers, to agree a framework for the content and style of the plan. Analysis by the Transition Officer of the time involved in this process indicated that, at that time (1996–97), each plan took two days from calling papers to final distribution.

The Transition Officer contacted all the agencies involved in the transition process and agreed calling procedures, and the commitment which each agency was prepared to make to facilitate the process, e.g.:

- Health: to arrange a medical examination around three months prior to the pupil's transition meeting and to given advice, if anything relevant to report.
- Careers: where possible a Careers Adviser to meet the pupil before the transition meeting and/or to attend the meeting.
- Social Services: to appoint a Transition Officer to work with the Education Transition Officer to coordinate assessment and review procedures and to attend specified transition meetings.
- Educational Psychologists: to submit advice where relevant and/or to attend the transition meeting.

From the SIMS database (an education management tool) a list of all pupils who would be 14 during the year 1996–97 was drawn up and these were allocated dates and times of meeting, either by the date the Statement was signed or by negotiation with the school. The dates and times of the transition reviews from January to July 1997 were distributed to SENCOs for comment and modifications were made. In consultation with the SENCOs and other agencies it was agreed that for the school year 1997–98 pupils whose birthdays fell between 30 June 1983 and 30 June 1984 would form the Post-14 Transition Group. This was for several reasons:

- those pupils whose birthdays fell in early July would be relatively immature and therefore less able to take full advantage of the process;
- those pupils whose birthdays fell during the summer holiday would be similarly disadvantaged;

- the existing excessive workload of annual reviews in June and July made drafting the Transition Plans difficult;
- to have schools vet the draft plans would not be possible until the following September.

A target was set to get the signed plans circulated within a month of the meeting. To rationalise the procedure it was agreed that all Post-14 Transition meetings would be driven by the Statement date so that they would be more evenly distributed during the year. This proved so successful that it has now been adopted by the whole Special Needs administration. Feedback from schools was also positive: most SENCOs found it more convenient to have their review workload spread throughout the year.

During the school year 1997–98 the process was modified to take into account certain anomalies which had arisen, such as parents not attending meetings, thus requiring a home visit. Schools were asked to alert the Transition Officer to those families where they had reason to believe that the parents were unlikely to attend, so that a home visit could be arranged in advance of the transition meeting. The parental invitation letter was amended so that more emphasis was put on the importance of a parental contribution – preferably in writing in advance of the meeting – with an offer of support from the Parent Partnership Officer/Transition Officer. This was taken up with considerable success.

The Transition Officer chaired the meeting, which incorporated the annual review, on behalf of the LEA. A standard set of questions was asked, based on the premise that the young person will eventually find him/herself in the world of work. The involvement of the Careers Service at this early stage helped focus the attention of the young person on areas of interest which could then be developed into relevant work experience placements. The plan would make specific recommendations regarding potential work experience and Post-16 opportunities.

During 1998 a joint-funded Transition Officer based in Health was appointed and also a joint-funded Transition Officer in conjunction with the Voluntary Sector. Main targets for the PPO were:

- to attend the annual reviews of out-of-borough pupils;
- to introduce a satisfaction survey (for pupils, parents, SENCOs and other relevant agencies);
- to locate and conduct meetings for pupils in Social Services-led out-of-borough placements;
- to locate and conduct meetings for young people in secure accommodation;
- to work with the Transition Officers Group on modifying the assessment and review process for transition.

Voluntary sector collaboration

The relationship between NCH (formerly National Children's Homes) and Walsall Parent Partnership Service dates back to 1993 when, in accordance with DfEE guidelines, a scheme was established which was accommodated partly at the Civic Centre, giving access to case-workers and files and partly at Walsall Resource Centre, giving an alternative, user-friendly, meeting place for parents and young people. A helpline was established, staffed by volunteers who were jointly recruited and trained by NCH and Parent Partnership. Volunteers were parents of children with special educational needs who had experience of the assessment process. Unfortunately some of these helpers moved to paid support work and some found the commitment too much while managing their families. However, the remaining helpers succeeded in maintaining the service with some help from the Resource Centre staff. Their work became more effective after the purchase of an updatable database which gives easy access to information on all disability and special needs issues and support groups and for which training for users was provided as part of the purchase package. The relationship between the two agencies has progressed apace. The Walsall Parent Partnership logo acknowledges the value of the joint working arrangement (see Figure 6.1).

The Parent Partnership Officer is a member of the NCH project committee and there is now a Service Level Agreement with NCH which covers recruitment, retention and management of volunteers, including IPSs; provision of office space and equipment at the Resource Centre; facilitation of monthly parent support group meetings; joint promotional presentations; provision of staff from both agencies to assist with newsletters and a room for half-termly editorial group meetings and shared space and expertise on websites. NCH manages the Joint Register of Children with a Disability for Walsall in conjunction with Education and Social Services.

Inclusion

The focus on inclusion through such initiatives as Standards Funding has impacted on the role of Parent Partnership Services. Category 2 of

Figure 6.1 The Walsall Parent Partnership logo

the DfES Standards Fund 2001–02 guidance states the purpose of funding for inclusion to be: 'To remove barriers to progress, address special educational needs and to promote social inclusion. In particular to reduce exclusion, raise attendance, provide full-time education for children out of school and address key social needs.' One of the objectives of this section is to 'support parent partnership and conciliation services for parents of children with special educational needs'.

In common with the majority of Parent Partnership Services, Walsall has become increasingly involved with the inclusion process, mediating between schools and parents and schools and the LEA. The service worked with colleagues from Social Services to set up an SEN parent forum, the 'Parent Voice', which is resourced through the voluntary sector Walsall Carers' Council so that it is completely independent of the local authority. This group feeds into the SEN Forum which is a strategic group representing all those with an interest in SEN. Those two groups have found that over some time inclusion (formerly integration) has had a major impact on developments in education practice in this country and elsewhere. The Salamanca Statement (UNESCO 1994) has also had a positive impact on the inclusion movement, though the issue remains contentious and there is a wide range of practice. Successful inclusion is the welcoming of all people as full members of their community, valuing them for their individual contribution. The diversity of their interests, abilities and achievements should be viewed as an enrichment of their local community, of which school will be a part. This view of inclusion is developed by Booth and Ainscow (1998) and the Index for Inclusion (CSIE 2000).

There is a diversity of opinion among LEA officers, teachers, parents and members of the DfES on this issue. One concern arising from the revised Code of Practice is that the emphasis seems to be on placing children with SEN in mainstream schools without suggestions for changing practice in such schools to make them inclusive communities. The response to Walsall's consultation document, which was circulated to all school governors and head teachers, was varied. It was viewed by some as a strategy to save the LEA money, to give children presently in special schools a second-rate education and to detract from the quality of education for children in mainstream schools: these arguments are discussed by Wilson (1999). Despite the reluctant acceptance of the empirical arguments for inclusion, namely, that children with SEN benefit socially and academically from mixing with their mainstream peers and that their peer group develops a better understanding of SEN issues, the majority of those involved in education in Walsall remain unconvinced about the practicalities of implementing inclusive practice.

For the Parent Partnership Service this has resulted in an increased caseload from parents of children at all stages on schools' SEN registers and from parents whose children are not being assessed but whose behaviour results in them being called in to remove their children from school, especially at lunchtimes. This is a regional and national trend.

Conflict resolution

Walsall PPS has been actively involved in conflict resolution since its inception in 1993 as this forms over 80 per cent of casework with parents and schools. There has been a regional PPS initiative in progress for two years which has resulted in a recent advertisement for an independent provider of mediation services for both the East and West Midlands who will train Parent Partnership Officers *and their managers* in the mediation process. For some time there has been an arrangement with NCH for Walsall PPS to use their case-workers, who are trained in conciliation, to undertake this function independently, should the need arise. There has been no such need. This is the result of training by the PPS for SEN caseworkers and other staff involved in direct contact with parents. The PPO was trained in mediation (Restorative Justice) by Thames Valley Constabulary. In 1999 there were 13 cases referred to the SEN Tribunal. Five of these were resolved by conciliation. In 2000 there were eight referrals, of which six were resolved by conciliation.

Service management

Initially, in common with the majority of services, Walsall PPS was managed by the Senior Inspector for SEN, a member of the LEA senior management team. Unfortunately there were several changes of SEN inspectors over a five-year period, each with consequent lengthy spells without a post-holder. As this caused significant procedural difficulties for the PPS, line management moved temporarily to the Group Coordinator for SEN. After a highly critical Ofsted inspection this post became redundant and, as an interim measure, management of the PPS passed to the Head of Assessment and Review Procedures Unit, who manages the caseworkers and Statements Officers. This caused concern from the outset as the dichotomy of running a service for parents at arm's length from the LEA while being managed by the head of the service against which most queries and/or complaints are likely to be addressed became increasingly apparent.

The Parent Partnership Service Development Plan outlines the key targets for the coming year and, in line with Best Value criteria, compares these with previous years' performance. Figure 6.2 is part of the current plan, showing how the service is addressing the five core activities of Parent Partnership plus arrangements for conflict resolution and how these relate to other key local authority plans.

The PPS budget and its management have long been a subject of concern to the PPO. Each year since 1999, when it was introduced, Walsall LEA has received its full quota of matched funding from the

1.0 NAME OF SERVICE			
Parent Partnership Service			

2.0 DESCRIPTION OF SERVICE			
2.1 Purpose of service			
To support parents and families of, and children with, SEN and to support schools in raising achievement, promoting inclusion and increasing access to learning for children with SEN in line with local and national developments.			

2.2 Key activities			
The DfES defines the five core activities of Parent Partnership Services as:		**% of service time spent on this:**	
• working with individual parents/families		40%	
• information and publicity		20%	
• training and support		20%	
• networking and collaboration		10%	
• helping to inform and influence local policy and practice.		5%	
There is also a requirement to develop a range of conflict resolution options to reduce the number of appeals to tribunal, including access to independent mediation services.			
		5%	

2.3 Activity indicators and performance review	**99/2000**	**2000/01**	**2001/02**
• **Working with individual parents/families**			
Number of referrals for parent support (casework) (conciliation)	66	126	
% increase			
Number of calls to the helpline	N/A	288	
of which 57 led to casework intervention	N/A	19.79%	
Access to database (by phone or appointment)	?	36	100
• **Information and publicity**			
Parent information booklet published	N/A	7.5K	
WALSEN newsletter – 2 issues	N/A	2 issues 9K	3 issues 13.5K
Publicity materials designed with NCH	N/A	1 presentation pack	2 new packs
Website design	N/A	Ongoing	Updated
Web page on NCH site	N/A	Complete	Updated
Newspaper article	N/A	1	3
Resource library	N/A	Ongoing	
Disability Awareness Event	1	1	3
Access to INCHES database (by phone or appointment)	?	36	100
Access to Internet for parents	N/A	N/A	3 facilities
	99/2000	**200/01**	**2001/02**
• **Training and support**			
Mentoring new PPOs in the Regional Network	4	2	?
Training sessions for school staff	1	3	9
Training sessions for school governors	N/A	2	6
Volunteer recruitment presentations	4	7	18
Training for IPSs	N/A	7	30
• **Networking and collaboration**			
Regional network meetings	6	6	
Regional network mediation/conflict resolution meetings	N/A	5	6
NPPN meetings	6	6	6
napps management meetings	5	6	6
SEC meetings	1	3	3
DfES consultation meetings	2	6	?
NCH project meetings	3	4	4

Child and Adolescent Mental Health steering group meetings	N/A	1	6
Deafblind steering group meetings	N/A	N/A	3
Equal Opportunities 'Education for All'	N/A	3	?
Education on the inter-agency Information Sharing Group	4	1	?
• **Helping to inform and influence local policy and practice**			
Youth Justice steering group meetings	6	4	6
Children with a Disability steering group meetings	6	6	6
Early Years and Childcare Partnership meetings	N/A	16	56
Early Years Business Partnership SEN meetings	N/A	3	6
Child and Adolescent Mental Health Steering group meetings	N/A	1	6
Deafblind steering group meetings	N/A	N/A	3
DfES consultation meetings	2	6	?
Equal Opportunities 'Education for All'	N/A	3	?
Access to independent mediation services			
Regional meetings to plan independent pilot	N/A	5	N/A
Monitoring of regional pilot	N/A	N/A	6
2.4 Links with key plans			
Education Development Plan			
Enabling parents access SEN provision to help improve attendance and reduce exclusion	N/A	27	100+
Consulting parents and young people			
Promoting inclusive practice	N/A		
Early Years Development Plan			
Early Years and Childcare Partnership meetings	N/A	16	56
Children with a Disability steering group meetings	6	6	6
Early Years Business Partnership SEN meetings	N/A	3	6
Behaviour Support Plan			
Weekly Multidisciplinary Behaviour Support Team meetings	N/A	N/A	40
Youth Justice Plan			
Youth Justice steering group meetings	6	4	6
Quality Protects			
Children with a Disability steering group meetings	6	6	6

Figure 6.2 Parent Partnership Service Development Plan 2001–02, March 2001

Standards Fund (formerly GEST), which has covered the core-funded salary of the PPO and travelling expenses.

The PPO attended conferences and training events organised by the NPPN at no cost and managed to keep abreast of regional and national initiatives by reading, by becoming involved in organising and contributing to such events and by representing Walsall and/or the West Midlands on such groups as the Special Education Consortium, the NPPN steering group, the NPPN policy group and **napps** (the National Association of Parent Partnership Services) of which she is a founder member.

Post-Ofsted the situation has improved somewhat.

Since the LEA is currently undergoing a restructuring in response to the Ofsted report, this would seem the ideal time review the financial allocation to the PPS.

The service is currently awaiting the outcome of our recent Best Value inspection. The feedback we have to date has been very positive.

Recommendations

The changing remit of the service

The Walsall Parent Partnership Service, which has been mainly involved in supporting families of children with Special Educational Needs, is now extending its service to parents who need help in any area of education other than curriculum (e.g. exclusions, social inclusion, bullying, relationships with school staff and/or the LEA).

(Quote from Chris Green, Director of Education and Community Services, in a letter to parent governors, 7 August 2001)

From January 2002 all LEAs are required to maintain a Parent Partnership Service which must meet minimum standards defined by the DfES in the Good Practice Toolkit which accompanies the new SEN Code of Practice (DfES 2001).

Greater involvement in schools

Through such initiatives as 'Parentaid' and through collaborative arrangements with other support services and governor training.

Inclusion

Developing training courses for parents and young people, working with colleagues from the Behaviour Support Team, the voluntary sector, Connexions, the Youth Justice Team and health and social services.

Conclusion

This chapter has described the evolution of Parent Partnership in Walsall, setting it in a regional and national context and identifying gaps in provision, examining how these were addressed and assessing the effectiveness of those which worked. Inevitably, in concentrating on key features of the changing nature of the service, there are areas which have not been covered.

Overall, recent legislation and advice from the government and other agencies have led to parents having a more informed and authoritative voice in the education process with more support networks and greater rights of appeal. The recent emphasis on inclusion for *all* children and on inclusive communities has resulted in a trend to educate more children in mainstream schools.

The negative factors for Parent Partnership nationally and locally include confusion over what exactly inclusion encompasses and how to empower parents and children in the education process without disenfranchising the existing power-brokers (including school staff).

References

Booth, T. and Ainscow, M. (1998) *From Them to Us: An International Study Of Inclusion In Education.* London: Routledge.

CSIE (2000) *Index for Inclusion: Developing Learning and Participation in Schools.* Bristol: Centre for Studies in Inclusive Education.

DfEE (1997) *Excellence for All Children: Meeting Special Educational Needs.* London: Department for Education and Employment.

DfEE (1998) *Meeting Special Educational Needs: A Programme of Action.* London: Department for Education and Employment.

DfES (2001) *SEN Code of Practice.* London: DfES.

UNESCO (1994) *World Conference on Special Educational Needs Education: Access and Quality.* Paris: UNESCO.

Wilson, J. (1999) 'Some conceptual difficulties about inclusion', *Support for Learning* **14**(3), 110–13.

Chapter 7

Parent Partnership Services in Islington: a strategic approach

Ann Braham

This chapter looks at the context and structure of Parent Partnership Services in the London Borough of Islington, the thinking and research that developed the theoretical framework of this strategic approach and at how it is being implemented. It begins by presenting an illustrative case study.

Empowering parents by access to information and to training

G, a young Turkish-speaking woman, joined the pilot course for parents/carers, 'A Guide to SEN', in the spring term 2001. As the very anxious parent of a young child starting the assessment procedure, she was delighted to find that the structure of this course allowed for discussions with other parents 'ahead' of her in the process.

The course content supported her with knowledge of the procedures and enhanced skills to deal with the issues involved. She continued to make the effort to travel into the borough to attend the course and receive support from the tutor and fellow students. G recently obtained a post as a bilingual Learning Support Assistant, having used her newly acquired knowledge of SEN issues at the job interview.

The Islington Parent Partnership Service (IPPS) did not set out with the intention of being an employment agency! However, this case is an effective illustration of the real empowerment of parents made possible by the decision to take a strategic rather than individual approach in Islington – an approach to Parent Partnership that presents many occasions for celebration and definite challenges.

Profile of the Borough of Islington

Islington covers roughly four square miles of London, just north of the City, with a population of approximately 176,000. It is characterised by the contrast between substantial wealth and great deprivation, some of the wards being the most deprived in England.

According to the borough's Children's Plan 1999–2002, there are 40,000 children and young people between the ages of 0 and 18 living in Islington, not all of whom attend the local schools.

The borough has 3 nursery schools, 9 Early Years Centres, 48 primary schools, 9 secondary schools, 4 special schools and 3 pupil referral units. Some 33 per cent of pupils have English as an additional language and 45 per cent have free school meals.

In April 2000, the Education Department (excluding the Early Years Service) was outsourced to a private company, CEA@Islington, and has recently passed an Ofsted inspection with flying colours.

The structure of the Parent Partnership Service

The present part-time coordinator (author of this chapter) was appointed in April 1999, at the beginning of the current Standards Fund initiative to provide support for Parent Partnership Services.

The steering group for this work is the Inclusion Advisory Group, which advises the Council on issues affecting children and young people, parents and carers concerning SEN. It includes strong representation of parents and voluntary organisations.

Line management is through the Head of Client Services (CEA@Islington) – services that include the SEN section, where the Parent Partnership Coordinator is part of a team working to support parents and carers with children with SEN. There are two officers specifically appointed with responsibility for consultation with parents concerning requests for statutory assessment and regarding statutory assessment, statements and pupil placement. The SEN section has recently been awarded a Charter Mark for the second time for its effective work with parents and other clients.

Much of the work of Parent Partnership is commissioned from independent organisations or organised with parent groups to achieve a degree of independence.

Current programmes

For parents

The Parent Partnership Service supports all events, talks and courses with resources for speaker, venue, crèche and refreshments.

Consultation
- Termly meetings of the SEN Forum; for example, on the proposed new SEN Framework for the borough – 'best consultation yet'; a parent's evaluation of this meeting.
- Focus group of parents.

Access to information and training
- Single issues talks – these are run jointly with the Parent Users Group, Camden and Islington Community Health Services NHS Trust, and take place once a month on areas of interest, e.g. autism, individual education plans, exclusions.
- Events run by the Ethnic Minority Achievement Service on the English Education System, including information on SEN.
- 'A Parents'/Carers' Guide to SEN' – an Open College Network accredited course commissioned from the Workers' Educational Association (WEA), a national voluntary training provider. The Level 1 course runs for 10×2 hours and is delivered once or twice a term, in different areas of the borough to enable easy access for parents. The Level 2 course is for students who want to become Independent Parent Supporters.

Access to Independent Parental Supporters (IPS)
- Access is via local groups with trained supporters such as Islington Parents of Children with SEN (IPCSEN) and the Communicative and Supportive Teaching/Learning Environment (CASTLE), and with community groups trained by the Advisory Centre for Education (ACE).

For schools and other education settings
- an information and advice pack;
- the Parent Support Register;

- offers of training bought in from Contact A Family (CAF) on setting up and maintaining Parent Support Groups and regular support to monitor the work;
- general consultancy and development work with schools on work to include parents;
- training through LEA courses; for example, an Inclusion Conference workshop for SENCOs and governors.

Conflict resolution

- A two-day mediation skills training and follow-up workshops for professionals to develop their skills in this area and to evaluate possible referrals to a formal service, offered, so far, to staff at CEA, Early Years and schools.
- Links to the London SEN Consortium for access to a formal service.

Making connections

- Building up networks and sharing good practice with schools, statutory agencies and voluntary organisations. For example, sharing information on individual support available from other parents of children with autism at a special school parent group; putting a head teacher in touch with the Access Officer to assess the possibility of wheelchair access in a three-storey Victorian school, following a request for help from a parent.
- Drawing other groups, such as local voluntary organisations, into the work so that the approach is coordinated and seamless.
- Providing a conduit for individual cases to IPS for advice and support.

Research which led to the key features and specialist areas of work

The theoretical framework

The Islington model for Parent Partnership takes a strategic rather than individual approach and aims to empower parents to be effective partners with schools and the Education Department in the education of their children with SEN. It is based on access to independent information and to training.

This strategic model also offers a consistent approach to the other elements in the coordinator's brief, which are to establish mediation arrangements for resolving disputes and a supportive, accessible network for both parents and professionals.

Key considerations in this work are – empowering parents, professionals and others to work more effectively together for the education of the children; removing barriers to inclusion; outsourcing the training for the 'independence element'; making offers that are practical and possible; early intervention and lifelong learning.

The research

The brief of the coordinator's post covered three main areas, which are derived from the proposals outlined in the Green Paper *Excellence for All Children* (DfEE 1997) and subsequent Programme of Action (DfEE 1998):

- to recruit, train and support Independent Parental Supporters (IPS) in consultation with schools;
- to establish conciliation arrangements, with an independent element, for resolving disputes with parents;
- to establish good communication with existing parent groups and voluntary organisations.

The obvious place to start was to look at the possible numbers of parents involved to get some idea of the scope of the work. The IPS were to be offered as support to parents and carers when their child is first identified as having SEN. Various sources put the numbers of children and young people living in the borough between ages 0–18 at approximately 40,000. If SEN runs at 20 per cent of the population – and the indicators suggest that it is probably higher – and each IPS works with four families, the Parent Partnership Coordinator would need to recruit, train and support between 2,000–3,000 volunteers to do the work effectively. Clearly, this was going to be interesting, but was it possible? Were there other ways of providing this support in the spirit of the Green Paper and Programme of Action? What are IPS meant to do? Could this be offered in another way, perhaps more effectively? Ideas, such as courses for parents, sprang to mind but needed to be checked out.

Wide-ranging discussions were held with other Parent Partnership Services such as that in Bradford coordinated by Barnardo's and other services suggested by the National Parent Partnership Network based at the National Children's Bureau.

Research also included publications such as the evaluation of previous Parent Partnership Schemes for the DfEE (Wolfendale and Cook 1997). This began to build up a picture of good practice in

Parent Partnership, which could be used to formulate a framework and evaluate progress in Islington.

At the same time, consultation began locally with the Education Department, the Early Years Service, schools, parents and voluntary organisations in the borough to find out what they wanted and how they saw the service developing. This consultation also began to build up networks and to research existing good practice in the borough.

Discussions with other projects using volunteers within the borough, for example, the Islington Home Start project and the special mentoring schemes in schools run by Education Welfare Officers, suggested that there were difficulties with recruitment *and* retention, as did the 1997 report from the National Centre for Volunteering (Smith 1997).

In Islington, there were already groups, part of the 'Education Advice Network' trained by the Advisory Centre for Education, who provided information and Named Persons. These groups, particularly IPCSEN, the local SEN parents group, confirmed the difficulties of the individual approach.

This message was particularly interesting from the local parent group who had difficulties recruiting volunteers even from among parents whom they had supported through the assessment process. The members of IPCSEN also made the point that a great deal of experience was needed by the volunteers, as well as training and support – 'it was at least a year with close supervision until I felt safe to support parents' – and that there were particular problems for volunteer IPS such as a minimum of 70 hours of work per case.

Meanwhile, the coordinator consulted other Parent Partnership Services on this specific area of work, including the Markfield Project in Haringey, which borders on Islington.

These organisations all agreed on the difficulties of recruitment and retention of volunteers. According to a London Parent Partnership Officer, among many others:

> We spend a lot of time and a huge amount of money on advertising across the authority. We get maybe 40 people ring up to express an interest. Twenty of them might turn up for the course and 10 manage to finish it. Only 3 are suitable for the work and 2 then get full-time jobs so you end up with just 1!

There were also clear messages from these sources that schools often found it difficult to cope with what they perceived as 'interference' from outside, when Named Persons come in to support parents. Some schools had also expressed a similar view so perhaps some school-based support to parents might be more acceptable. But to balance the needs of parents and schools could be like walking a tightrope!

From this research, it became clear that IPPS should take a different approach informed by good practice and the borough's Life Long Learning programme. It would be a strategic rather than individual approach, working through schools with information packs and parent support groups, offering training to empower parents, with formal access to IPS for the more complex cases. This particular approach also works for conflict resolution, with training in Mediation Skills for all and access to the London SEN Consortium's formal service for complex cases. The schools and parents consulted were happy with this approach.

Key features and specialist areas of work

These are supporting schools to work more effectively with parents and provide them with information, advice and support; empowering parents by access to information and training; and developing a 'climate of mediation' – a positive approach to problem solving. These are all underpinned by effective networking.

Working with schools – information, advice and individual/personal support

This approach builds on the good relations of the coordinator with most of the schools, through other work within the Learning Support Service. It is important for long-term success that schools take responsibility for this work with parents – that it is not just an add-on (like the responsibility for SEN!).

Schools are also the key distributors of the flyers for the consultations, talks and for the WEA course to the parents and carers.

The Parent Partnership Service has prepared two key documents to help meet the expectation that parents should have effective support, including access to independent advice, from the earliest stage at which their child's SEN is identified. These documents are an information and advice reference pack on SEN issues and the Parent Support Register.

Information and advice packs

Every school has an information pack to support parents. The information mainly covers local organisations for SEN, community groups and support groups, although many national organisations have their headquarters in or near Islington and so have been included. It is regularly updated and expanded, although it is important to keep it manageable. Information from some websites is included, for example, from 'Young Minds' – to make clear the kind of support offered by that group. When a child's needs are identified, the SENCO can provide parents with information on how to access independent advice from the pack.

The Parent Support Register

The SENCOs in all schools and Early Years Centres have been given a Parent Support Register. This is a key document in addressing the issue of IPS in the spirit of the Programme of Action rather than by recruiting individuals as it introduces a more human and personal element into the support rather than just sharing a website address or the phone number of an organisation.

The register is quick and simple to use – important for busy SENCOs – and makes formal what one or two schools are already doing. It is to be used alongside the SEN register and can be used in several ways.

Register headings

Name/s of Parent Supporter	Main area of interest in SEN	Child on Support or Support plus	How to contact Parent Supporter	Consent of Parent Supporter

Some schools intend to use it to provide parent-to-parent support on specific disabilities. For instance, a new pupil with Down's Syndrome joins the school. When the SENCO gets to know the parents, they could be asked to join the register. The SENCO would record information about this on the register and use it when appropriate. If another child joins the school with the same disability, the parents on the register would talk to the parents of the new pupil about how the school works and how their child manages.

Some schools are intending to use it for recording an offer of support from four or five parents whose children have more general special needs or indeed from parents who would like to be actively involved in the school but whose children do not have SEN. In fact, both approaches would work together. The offer of support is made when a pupil is new or when the special educational need is first identified.

Parent Support Groups – the 'human element'

Schools are being supported with training from CAF and advice from the coordinator to establish and/or develop and maintain school-based support groups. At one of the special schools, the outreach teacher set up a parent support group after attending the course. 'The course enabled me to focus on the issues involved and to share things that had worked in other schools. It also had practical ideas for setting up a parent support group . . . the one in our school is still going strong a year after it started.' The monthly meetings have built up to 12–15 regular members who have decided to work on their communication and assertion skills as well as meet informally to chat and exchange information on how to access their disability rights.

In some schools, parent groups have naturally arisen out of an activity, for example, the Islington Language and Communication Team worked with parents at a primary school on games and activities to do at home with the children. These parents want to continue to meet as a group and the Parent Partnership coordinator is advising the school on this issue.

In other schools, the parents identified on the Parent Register are encouraged to become the core of a Parent Support Group for the school. In such a group, these parents can also find support for themselves.

The use of the Parent Register and the support groups enables the school to provide parent supporters from within their own setting and thus addresses the issue of providing IPS when schools do not like 'outside interference'. Should the issues become too complex or difficult for school-based support, there are independent groups in Islington, like IPCSEN, which can provide that more formal support.

Training for professionals

The Parent Partnership Service provides training to those working with parents. This offers quality and structured thinking time and the exchange of ideas on good practice. For example, on a locally delivered module of the London Institute of Education's Diploma in SEN, the materials emphasised the development of positive attitudes to parents, user-friendly information and procedures and encouraged an awareness that parents are not a homogeneous group.

Information and advice

The Parent Partnership Service together with the Parent User group has set up a series of monthly talks on issues of SEN for parents and carers, professionals and anyone else interested. The annual programme covers a wide range of issues and the speakers are chosen by the parents, to maintain a degree of independence.

Parents commented after one talk – 'lots of information delivered in a friendly way', 'inspiring' and 'lots of information giving me more power to help my child'. An unexpected benefit is the interesting mix of the audience, with workers from health and education as well as parents. Those from health commented on how useful it was for them to hear the parents' point of view.

Courses for parents

The importance of training for parents was emphasised in the Draft revised Code of Practice (DfEE 2000). It is one of the five key areas expected of Parent Partnership Services. The IPPS could deliver a high quality course but did not want to develop and tutor a course because this might not be considered as independent enough from the LEA for some parents. There was a need to find one elsewhere that was acceptable and of a high standard.

At the NPPN course for new coordinators, Roger Parnell, from the WEA South Western District Parent Partnership Service, described a course that fitted the requirements exactly. The course both gives detailed information on SEN and develops the skills of the students to deal effectively with professionals. There is an expectation that parents will eventually become course tutors (see Chapter 8).

The WEA in the south-west developed this course during the first incarnation of Parent Partnership Services. The WEA was hoping to roll the course out across the country with DfEE support and Islington became the first area for this development.

In the spring term 2001, the London WEA Family Learning Section ran the pilot course in the Central Library after intensive work to customise it for the borough and to update the look of it. The parents who joined the course were informed that it was a pilot and invited to be part of the team evaluating it. The fact that eight of the ten students who started the course continued to the end – the two who left got full-time jobs! – suggests that this course is successfully fulfilling a need. The comments of the parents clearly indicate just how useful they found this course.

Thanks to the course, I was much better informed.
> (A parent going through the statementing process
> with a child aged 3 with complex needs)

It gave access to good information and where you get it from.
> (The parent of a child with dyslexia in a primary mainstream school)

I was less anxious – it was a GODSEND – hearing from people who had been through it.
> (The parent of a boy aged 4 with general difficulties
> at the beginning of the assessment process)

Good to have empowerment ourselves, not just to have an Independent Parent Supporter given to us, so that we can cope when people like LEA officers ring us unexpectedly at home.
> (The same parent)

Other useful features, according to the parents, were the discussions with other parents, an encouraging, sympathetic and flexible tutor and hearing other people's perspective from visiting professionals. The tutors enjoy it too. It is encouraging to find that after just two terms, parents are already showing an interest in becoming tutors themselves.

Conflict resolution

Thinking and research on this task led to the same over-arching and strategic approach – to work better together to obviate the need for dispute. Some elements are common, for example, offering a programme to provide parents with information and empower them as well as offering training to schools and LEA on mediation skills and other good practice.

The DfEE publication *Resolving Disputes between Parents, Schools and LEAs: Some Examples of Best Practice* confirms the effectiveness of this 'early intervention' approach based on training (Hall 1999: 19–20).

The Parent Partnership Service commissioned Zanne Findlay and Akin Thomas, both well-known trainers in this field, to deliver a series of training sessions and workshops to develop and enhance the skills of those working with parents. The training would also enable participants to evaluate cases for formal mediation when that service was established. This training was first offered to the LEA officers in the SEN section, the Educational Psychology Service, the Education Welfare Service and to the Early Years Service officers, and then to include staff in schools and Early Years Centres.

However, the coordinator's work with the primary and secondary lead Learning Mentors, funded from Excellence in Cities, on joint training for Learning Support Assistants and for Learning Mentors, led to a huge uptake of the mediation training by the mentors in both phases.

What has worked well (or not) with reasons

Some challenges

- With the current emphasis on inclusion, schools need to take responsibility for working with parents, for instance, they often want Parent Partnership Services to run groups or talks for them.
- It is often difficult to get good practice established in schools as changing staff can mean starting over again.
- One of the major challenges of this strategic approach is that it may feel slow to start and publicity can be difficult; reaching parents at Stages 1–3 often depends on a busy SENCO.
- Connections and networking – there is so much going on that it is often difficult to keep an overview but great when it enables connections to be made.
- There are issues common to all Parent Partnership Services, which will need addressing – the limited time in which to carry out the work and the financial wherewithal so to do.
- Secondary schools are more difficult to involve in this work, partly because of the normal tendency of parents to withdraw from close involvement at school as children get older. A model is being tried out, based on a telephone network for specific disabilities.
- Running events with parents of children with SEN can often be more time consuming than expected as children have first call on parents' time.
- There are some indicators of success in trying to build a 'climate of mediation' in the borough. One of the participants in the mediation course has become one of the London Consortium mediators and one has successfully mediated in a secondary school where he works on crime reduction. The Complaints Officers from Social Services have asked to join the next mediation skills course. The PPS, working with CEA@Islington's Exclusions Officer, hopes to build on these small beginnings to offer mediation to schools as an alternative positive way to resolve issues between schools, pupils and parents – quite a challenge!

Celebrations

- 'Parent Partnership is developing well' Ofsted Report on Islington, March 2001.
- There is a growing number of successful school-based parent groups – the special school group mentioned earlier is now going to become two, one group for each phase.
- The WEA course is gathering momentum – 60 parents/carers have expressed an interest in the next course being held in the north of the borough, four times the number who attended the borough-wide pilot course. The evaluations are excellent – parents are feeling emotionally supported and empowered – and the first parent tutor is about to be trained.
- In the second year of the talks, numbers attending are increasing and many of the evaluations ask for more.
- Perhaps the greatest cause for celebration is the fact that parents themselves are feeling empowered to take the lead in many of the activities, particularly in schools. They are also beginning to be active in spreading the word about the talks and the courses on offer.

Where next? Building on success

There are several indicators for future work in the previous section. Some of these will depend on networking, sharing good practice and making connections, for example, encouraging schools on board, developing work with Social Services and developing a climate of mediation. Some of them are very practical, such as setting up a Parent Centre with information and Internet access and translating the WEA course for ethnic community groups. Others may evolve organically, for example, the focus group taking a more active role and parents taking over running groups, organising talks, and so on.

The new Code of Practice lays out five key areas for the minimum standards in Parent Partnership and mentions 'empowering parents to play an informed and active part in their child's education', and 'a menu of flexible services'. It emphasises the importance of training for parents and professionals. These indicators fit well with the approach taken to Parent Partnership in Islington.

References

DfEE (1997) *Excellence for All Children*. London: DfEE.
DfEE (1998) *Meeting SEN: A Programme of Action*. London: DfEE.

DfEE (2000) *Draft Revised Code of Practice on the Identification and Assessment of Pupils with SEN*. London: DfEE.

Hall, J. (1999) *Resolving Disputes between Parents, Schools and LEAs: Some Examples of Best Practice*. London: DfEE.

Smith, D. (1997) *The 1997 National Survey of Volunteers*. London: National Centre for Volunteers.

Wolfendale, S. and Cook, G. (1997) *Evaluation of SEN Parent Partnership Schemes*. DfEE Research Report No. 34. London: DfEE.

Young Minds, accessible at: www.youngminds.org.uk

Chapter 8

Joined up working: perspectives on the development of Parent Partnership Services in the South West of England

Sheila Clarkson, Roger Parnell and Christopher Onions

Introduction

This chapter provides three individual perspectives on the development of a Parent Partnership Scheme in the South West of England, from an LEA, GEST-funded project to one which is now freestanding of an LEA but able to work closely with a number of LEAs. It provides an account of the challenges and changes which the original Parent Partnership Project in Devon faced following the ending of GEST funding in 1997, local government reorganisation (April 1998) and the reintroduction of funding for such schemes through Standards Fund in support of the Programme of Action (DfEE 1998). It focuses on the current structure and organisation of the scheme using one LEA as a specific example of good practice.

The transition phase – Sheila Clarkson

The context and background to this project have been described elsewhere (Trier 1997) but a brief summary of the key developments are required to provide a framework for the subsequent evolvement described here.

The Devon scheme had hoped to establish, by the end of the GEST-funded period, an organisation for parents and carers that was freestanding of the LEA, with an assured funding route. One approach, considered in conjunction with parents and representatives of the LEA, was to develop an organisation, registered as a charity in its own right, which would be governed and managed by those parents and carers who were actively involved in supporting the project. This proposal met with little enthusiasm. Parents and carers expressed concerns that they already had busy enough lives without the added responsibility that such a development would bring. The clear message was that they valued having a third party who could act on their behalf. No solution had been found by December 1996, with GEST funding due to expire in March 1997. Devon LEA was not unsupportive and agreed to maintain sufficient funding for a further ten months (i.e. until January 1998) for the four 0.5 fte (full-time equivalent) area project worker posts, as they were seen to be essential to the coordination and support of the 'Special Partner' network. This funding also ensured continuity of the work in the lead-up to local government reorganisation in April 1998 when Devon was restructured, with Plymouth and Torbay being established as new, unitary authorities.

The Devon project had identified the need for parents to have access to accurate information and support from an early point in time and had extended the Named Person role, in essence pre-empting the Independent Parental Supporter (IPS) role identified in the Programme of Action (DfEE 1998). IPS was (and is) provided through 'Special Partners', many of whom are parents/carers of children with special needs. The training for these volunteers was well established and an additional training course for all parents and carers had also been developed. This latter course was designed to offer a general introduction to the topic of Special Educational Needs from which basis interested parents and others could progress to the Special Partner training course. Accreditation for the courses was considered to be important both in giving recognition to those people who completed them and in showing that volunteers were valued by the project. Routes were being explored with the Open College Network (OCN) when Trier (1997) was being written but were not finalised. The project's lack of permanence was a major stumbling block. OCN required the courses to be 'held' by an organisation which could guarantee their continuation if funding for the project was unavailable. Initially it was intended to link these courses to a portfolio of others provided by Parent Education in Devon and already accredited by OCN. This proved not to be feasible but it was suggested that the Workers Educational Association (WEA) might consider these courses as being suitable for delivery under their umbrella. The WEA proved to be helpful and interested and both courses were accredited early in 1997. A number of experienced adult education tutors interested in special educational needs were trained to deliver the course.

During the final three months of GEST funding the County Steering Group recognised the need to explore alternative funding routes. Nationally at this time, the future existence of Parent Partnership Schemes was in the balance, with some schemes reported as discontinued. Following a number of conversations with the Devon Special Projects Officer, it became apparent that there were only two possible sources of funding whose criteria fitted with the work of the project, a

National Lottery Commission Grant (deadline March 1997) or a grant from the Nuffield Foundation (deadline July 1997). Both avenues seemed like a long shot, complicated by the fact that the project was seen to be a part of a statutory organisation and not independent in its own right. A tentative approach was made to the WEA to consider whether it might be interested in taking on the wider remit of the project as it was already holding the accredited training courses. A very positive response was received from the WEA, which as an organisation, offered three key features that would enable it to help the Parent Partnership Project achieve its objectives:

- The WEA as an association of voluntary members already had substantial experience in the development of voluntary networks.
- The WEA as a provider of adult education programmes was in a position to provide continuing support for the parent and volunteer training programmes.
- The WEA as an independent charity would be able to provide the expertise in the establishment of the Parent Partnership Project into a formally constituted organisation to secure its long-term viability.

The proposal that the WEA should submit a bid on behalf of the project was subsequently taken to the County Steering Group who saw the advantages as being that:

- The WEA would offer a no-cost solution if the funding was achieved and could provide a route to becoming an independent charitable organisation.
- There would be a tight deadline if the project was to become a charity in its own right before January 1998 and then funding opportunities would be missed.
- There was agreement that going under the umbrella of the WEA was useful both in terms of funding bids (being the National Lottery in the first instance) and the general evolution of the project.

The most significant change the proposal would bring related to the WEA's remit as their South West District covers both Devon and Cornwall. From their perspective it was considered inappropriate to submit a bid on behalf of Devon only. It was sad but fortuitous that Cornwall LEA had decided not to continue funding Parent Partnership work as this created a vacuum which the WEA was in a position to fill. The bid which was submitted had three outline project objectives:

- continued development of the voluntary network;
- continued development of appropriate support systems for parents and carers of children who have special educational needs;
- continued recruitment and training of volunteers to support the network.

It seemed against all the odds that the WEA National Lottery bid was successful. One final task remained. This was to ensure that all newly appointed staff were familiar with the Special Partner training course and able to run it. A 'Training for Trainers' course was delivered by the original Devon Parent Partnership Project team in April 1998 ensuring that the volunteer course could be offered across the South West region.

The involvement of the voluntary sector – Roger Parnell

The autumn of 1997 was a time of celebration! A champagne bottle popped on the news of this successful National Lottery bid of £353,463 – the largest award in the South West at the time. Parent Partnership was set to continue for a further three years and work previously carried out with so much dedication and commitment could now be continued.

The project had moved from a statutory to a voluntary sector provider and furthermore, much of the good practice and structures developed in Devon were to be extended into Cornwall and a new two-county project. Apart from meeting the WEA criteria for offering a two-county service consistent with its South Western District, there were other clear advantages. For example, in extending Parent Partnership across a wider area, there would be more opportunities to support and involve a greater number of parents in this exciting development.

Over a period of time, the formation of seven area steering groups (some of which were already in existence), and one new Regional Steering Group, would ensure that communication between parent representatives and professionals across the region would be maintained. Our steering groups have proved to be an excellent example of partnership working and involve parents, LEAs and members from other statutory and voluntary organisations.

A parent of two children with special educational needs, and a member of our Regional Steering Group, spoke of the value of such groups. She said: 'The whole set-up is an oasis of good feeling, mutual understanding and of professionals sharing their knowledge willingly and enthusiastically to enable children and their families to get the best out of life'. But it had taken a while to reach this stage.

Early barriers to progress

Following the transition from Devon LEA to the WEA, one problem dominated proceedings. For some, the organisational change was unwelcome. Issues surrounding employment, confidentiality, data collection of parental enquiries, volunteer travel rates, working areas and the sharing of Parent Partnership between two counties, made for some difficult and challenging early days. It was a time of listening carefully to parents, staff and other professionals, often in heated debate.

In reality, this was a new two-county project with new, external funding under the umbrella of a new organisation. In practice, to help reduce the perceived threat of this change and begin working towards an acceptance of the moving on process, a 'continuation' of the project in Devon, had to be balanced against what was a 'new' project in Cornwall. It was a unique situation for all involved and it would take time before many of these early issues could be resolved.

During this early period, local government reorganisation meant that Parent Partnership also needed to adapt to these changes. Parent Partnership Services were not a legal requirement for LEAs in 1998, although in time, each LEA would emerge with its own Parent Partnership agenda and policies. Although some professionals raised doubts about the WEA's ability to deliver a Parent Partnership Service, this was counter-balanced by support and belief from others. However, confidence between the WEA and each of the four LEAs still needed to be built, maintained or restored, whichever was the case.

The first 12 months contained upheaval and challenge, but the WEA Parent Partnership continued to grow by supporting more parents, offering more training and increasing its volunteer IPS base. Our focus was to ensure that parents remained at the core of our service, and we aimed to achieve this by continuing to offer two key benefits:

1. To provide information and support for parents who requested it.
2. To provide opportunities for those same parents to become involved in Parent Partnership work, either as trained volunteers, steering group members or part-time tutors.

These opportunities would help parents to develop new skills and knowledge in the company of other parents and become more confident when working with their children's schools or the LEAs. The main beneficiaries would be the parents themselves, other parents, professionals and most importantly, the children.

A comment from a parent in Cornwall, who attended one of our Parent Partnership training courses, best illustrates the benefit of this approach. She wrote: 'I have gained so much knowledge regarding special educational needs, and being a parent of a child with special educational needs, I feel I can now approach professionals with understanding and far less stress.' This was sharply contrasted, on another occasion, by the view of one professional, who stated: 'The more parents know, the more tribunals there will be.' The key issue here is not just about giving information to parents. It's about our ability to support them through the processes, and this is what our teams of development workers, tutors and IPSs set out to achieve. Parent Partnership had to be from the parents outwards and not from the LEAs downwards, although both still needed to work together as equal partners in the process.

Training: how we are successfully developing and maintaining our IPS Network

Across Devon, Cornwall, Plymouth and Torbay, in addition to our seven development workers, there are now 15 qualified part-time tutors and seven additional tutors in training. Many of our tutors are parents of children with special educational needs who have progressed from making an initial enquiry relating to their child, to successfully completing the City and Guilds 7307 Adult and Further Education Teaching Certificate, parents supporting and training other parents. It is through this model of parent enquiries and training that we have recruited our IPSs.

The Revised Code of Practice 2001 [2:15] states: 'The voluntary sector has a unique and important contribution to make in supporting parents.' In the South West, there is clear evidence that the WEA, as a voluntary organisation and adult education provider, continues to play an important part in the growth area of Parent Partnership work and IPS training and development. Part of this success is attributed to our two-tiered accredited training programme:

1. A Parents/Carers Guide to Special Educational Needs – This course provides parents, carers, learning support assistants, school governors and others with an opportunity to acquire a basic knowledge and understanding of special educational needs and of the increasing role played by Parent Partnership Services.

2. Supporting Parents and Carers of Children with Special Educational Needs – Our IPS training course which provides participants (most of whom are parents), with some of the skills needed to support other parents and carers of children with special educational needs.

Although not a compulsory progression route, the majority of our volunteers have attended both courses. Our original training programmes, designed by the Devon Parent Partnership team, and accredited in 1997 through the Open College Network, have enabled over 1,200 parents to take part in training. From this base, we have developed and maintained an average of between 80 and 100 active IPSs over a three-year period – a credit to the skills and commitment of those volunteers and our development workers who recruit, train and support them.

Our volunteer numbers are relatively high, but as with other areas, we have experienced recruitment difficulties. Many potential volunteers live in isolated areas and can be affected by bad weather, lack of transport and lack of time, especially if they have demanding family commitments. Therefore, when we are fortunate to have their services, we know we must value their time and commitment, and support them accordingly. In order to do this, we first have to ask and understand the answers to the question: 'Why do people volunteer?' The reasons are varied and individual. Yet we need to support volunteers according to their own unique reasons as to why they want to volunteer. This gives us the best chance of retaining their valuable services.

However, although volunteers offer their services free of charge, the ongoing support for them does not come free. It takes a great deal of development worker time and resources to fully undertake the level of support and training needed to maintain an IPS network. Most of our development workers are part-time and carry out other development work as part of a job that frequently involves mid- to long-distance travel. It is a difficult balance between needs, development worker time, available budget and the expectation of others. Volunteer development has been a grossly under-funded area of Parent Partnership work, considering the important role and responsibility given to IPSs and those who are expected to recruit, train and support them.

We should also consider the time and care needed to support individual parents, some of whom are desperate just to speak to someone who will listen and help. It is often a case not of how many parent enquiries we receive in one day, but how we have given those parents the quality time, information and support they have needed, acknowledging too, the individual abilities or difficulties some parents may have in supporting their own children.

Where are we now?

Since our National Lottery funding ended in December 2000, service agreements have been made between the WEA and each of the four LEAs of Cornwall, Devon, Plymouth and Torbay. In Devon, education, health and social services within a Primary Care Trust structure jointly fund a new WEA Parent Partnership Service, therefore widening our previous LEA remit.

Our two training courses have been re-designed and are again accredited through the Open College Network South West. Parents, development workers, tutors and LEA Parent Partnership representatives have all contributed to the re-writing and presentation of the new material, giving courses which can be transferred with confidence to other WEA Districts and ultimately offered to parents and LEAs across the UK.

Our development workers are emerging into self-managing teams. Each one is an outreach worker who has developed his or her own skills and styles within a WEA Parent Partnership framework. It is important that this process continues as it motivates, empowers, encourages responsibility, develops personal skills, and encourages trust and support within the team.

The WEA Parent Partnership Service in the South West is meeting an important need in parent/carer support, training and IPS development, and our track record as a voluntary sector provider, in partnership with parents and LEAs in this important area of work, is now being nationally recognised.

The Plymouth approach – Christopher Onions

Since local government reorganisation in 1998, Plymouth has continued to develop its own model of service delivery for Parent Partnership. In this, we have been aided by a LEA that has seen a *genuine* partnership with parents as a real asset rather than a threat. My own title and position of 'Parent Partnership Support Leader' reflects the Plymouth approach. As an Educational Psychologist with the Plymouth LEA, I am employed for two days a week to work *with* the Plymouth Parent Partnership Service. I do *not* run it. The aim has been to develop a partnership where the LEAs policies, funding and decision-making processes are made transparent to parents. We have started from the belief that parents and professionals have the same common aims – the best interests of the child. While difficulties may sometimes arise in providing exactly what a parent requests, as a result of limited resources or limitations in the way the system currently operates, negotiated agreement is, at the end of the day, a fairer and more effective means of addressing these difficulties than confrontation. It also permits the growth of positive dialogue between parents and professionals which, over time, will lead to two-way understanding and better services for all. The cooperative structure of the Plymouth service is outlined in Figure 8.1.

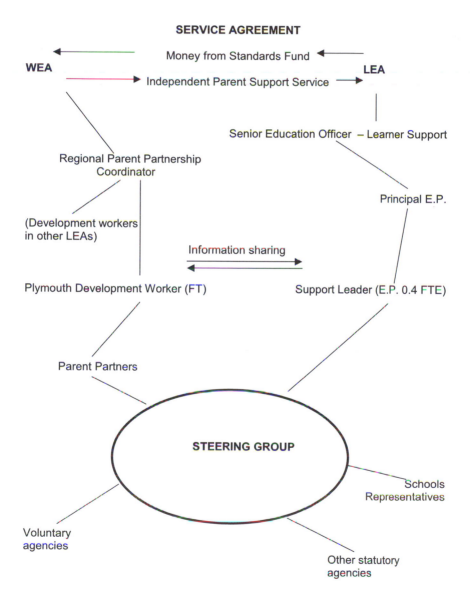

Figure 8.1 Plymouth Parent Partnership – service structure

Management and funding

The service is run, on a day-to-day basis, by the development worker who is employed and managed by the WEA. Money is paid by the LEA, from Standards Fund, to the WEA, for an agreed service which includes: appointment and management of the development worker; management of the volunteer Parent Partners; premises; training; production of information, etc. In this way, the independence of the service from the LEA is maintained. My role is to liaise with the Parent Partnership Service and to ensure that they have access to all the information they need in order to understand how services in Plymouth operate. When asked, I also provide the development worker with information, which will help Parent Partners in supporting parents with particular needs. I also have a brief from the LEA to promote the use of Parent Partnership by schools and to help schools to develop positive partnerships with parents.

Accountability and influence

The service is accountable to a steering group, which is always chaired by a parent. This group is comprised of representatives of the main agencies – Education, Social Services and Health – and other groups, including voluntary groups, involved with parents and children. The number of parents always exceeds the number of professionals. Meetings are held approximately every six weeks. As well as receiving a report from the development worker on work undertaken and issues arising, the group provides a forum through which parents are able to represent their views and concerns directly to the representatives of the statutory agencies. It has also begun to provide a forum within which new ideas from statutory agencies, likely to affect parents and children, are discussed and modified in the light of parental feedback. For example, the Senior Education Officer in charge of Learner Support recently came to talk over with parents proposals to change the way in which funding for special needs is allocated within the authority. Parents' concerns over the accountability of head teachers for devolved special needs funding were duly taken into account. While obviously not yet representative of all parents, this dialogue has the potential to provide a way for parents to become actively involved in the planning and decision-making processes of the LEA and other statutory agencies. Increasingly, parents from Plymouth Parent Partnership are being asked to contribute to the development and work of other initiatives such as the Early Years Partnership and the Connexions service, targeted at the adolescent years.

Work of the service

Table 8.1 shows the steady growth in demand for the service and the types of enquiry made and the support given. The increase in enquiries reflects the growing success of the service as parents, who have been helped and supported, tell others. Over the past three years no Plymouth parent has felt the need to appeal to a Special Needs Tribunal. While other factors are involved, for example, the 'parent aware' attitudes of special needs staff in the LEA, there is no doubt that the Plymouth Parent Partnership Service has been able to make a significant contribution to helping parents and the LEA to negotiate rather than confront.

Like most Parent Partnership projects we started with the aim of providing independent information and support to parents who had a child with special educational needs. We always took the view that this should be at any stage of the old Code of Practice (DFE 1994). This broad view has been broadened still further in response to what parents want – a one-stop shop that is capable of supporting them and signposting them to the services they need for themselves as parents and their children. Parent Partners may accompany parents to meetings with health professionals or social services. We have Parent Partners who are trained to assist parents in making claims for Disability Living Allowance. At an early meeting with Plymouth parents of children with special needs, held soon after local

Table 8.1 Enquiries to Plymouth Parent Partnership Services, 1998–2000

Main reason for contact	1998	1999	2000
Accompany to, support at, and preparation for meetings	54	100	111
Annual Review	9	24	26
Code of Practice procedures	30	53	64
General support	167	231	259
Information on courses	6	28	31
Proposed statement	20	37	25
Provision	38	63	95
Seek information	11	33	49
Direct help given			
Help with written contribution	17	24	21
Home visit	20	46	39
Information given by telephone	166	275	397
Professional contacted for parent	16	43	55
Referred to special partner for support	68	135	132
Sent PPPS information pack	26	22	55
Total enquiries	182	298	425

government reorganisation, the vast majority of parents made it very clear that while they wanted support for their children's special needs, they preferred this to be part of a service that offered support to all parents. In response to this and in order to reflect the move towards more inclusive thinking in education, we have broadened what we do to offer information and support, not just to parents of children with special educational needs but to parents of *all* children, over such issues as exclusion, school entry preferences, secondary school preferences, bullying, etc. The change of name for our volunteers from Special Partners to Parent Partners mirrors this shift towards a more inclusive perspective.

Looking to the future

We would like to see the Plymouth Parent Partnership Service continue to develop a range of information and support for all parents in Plymouth – a sort of Citizens Advice Bureau for all parenting related issues. We would like to see it developing to become part of a fully-fledged parenting forum for Plymouth, where parents can have the opportunity to be involved with professionals, on an ongoing basis, in the strategic planning of the services that affect them and their children. But this means a significant increase in the number of Parent Partners. We currently have 19 active volunteers in Plymouth. While we have no great difficulties in being able to recruit more volunteers, volunteers need to be managed and supported. Our full-time development worker can just about manage our existing service. In order to develop, we need additional paid staff to train and support a greater number of volunteers. The goodwill of volunteers cannot be taken for granted. A significant factor in retaining volunteers is high quality professional support, information and opportunities for additional training, which give them the confidence and feeling of being valued that will maintain motivation doing what can be a very demanding job.

The announcement that LEAs would have a statutory duty to ensure that parents in their areas have access to a Parent Partnership Service from 1 January 2002 was welcome news. This takes away some of the financial insecurity that has dogged the provision and development of these services to date but it introduces new concerns. With no 'ring-fencing', as there was under Standards Funding, how generous will LEAs be in making provision for these services from their core budgets with so many other competing priorities? We are likely to see wide disparities between those LEAs with a real commitment to Parent Partnership and those who go for providing the 'minimum standards' as set down in the Revised Code of Practice (DfES 2001).

Summary

The involvement of an outside, voluntary body, the WEA, as the umbrella organisation managing the services and providing high quality training, has enabled the LEAs involved (Devon, Torbay, Plymouth and Cornwall) to develop Parent Partnership Services that are seen to be independent in the information and support they offer parents. The separate service agreements with the individual LEAs have ensured that each LEA has a service that reflects the needs of its individual area. The involvement of the WEA has also brought expertise in training and managing volunteers that has enabled a strong and mutually supportive network of services to be built up across the South West, with best practice being shared across the region.

References

DFE (1994) *Code of Practice on the Identification and Assessment of Special Educational Needs.* London: Stationery Office.

DfEE (1998) *Excellence for All Children: Meeting Special Educational Needs: A Programme of Action.* London: DfEE.

DfES (2001) *Revised Special Educational Needs Code of Practice.* London: DfES.

Trier, S. (1997) 'Promoting the effective practice of partnership', in Wolfendale, S. (ed.) *Working with Parents of SEN Children After the Code of Practice.* London: David Fulton Publishers.

Chapter 9

Independence and empowerment: Independent Parental Support as an integral component of a support structure for parents in Essex

Jill Lloyd

Introduction

The purpose of this chapter is to provide an overview of the development of the Independent Parental Supporter (IPS) scheme operated by Families InFocus (Essex), a relatively young charity based in Chelmsford, Essex. The editor approached me to write this chapter to look at Parent Partnership specifically from the viewpoint of an organisation run by parents for parents. This parental perspective therefore is of the IPS scheme rather than the wider LEA-operated Parent Partnership Services (PPS). However, I would like to acknowledge the constructive comments made by Essex LEA in its drafting.

The background and context enable the reader to understand the rationale behind the development of the scheme. The underpinning values are examined in the context of independence and partnership. It explores the evolving relationship between an independent voluntary organisation and its LEA, how tensions may arise and how these may be averted and resolved. IPS is seen as an integral component of an holistic scheme whose remit extends beyond the sphere of special educational needs.

With the majority of the trustees of Families InFocus (Essex) being parents of children with special needs, the scheme has drawn on their strengths and experiences. In line with a key responsibility of PPS, the LEA has developed close working relationships with many local voluntary organisations and since 1999 has chosen to provide the IPS service by contracting this out to Families InFocus (Essex).

Background and context

As a result of an in-depth study by a multi-agency joint planning group for children with disabilities in Mid-Essex (i.e. the local authority areas of Braintree, Chelmsford and Maldon), Families InFocus (Essex) was set up in 1996. Requests for support from the charity started flooding in when an office base was established the following February. At the end of the first year of full operation, an analysis of the work undertaken with families pointed to at least 25 per cent of this revolving around education issues. The Director, author of this chapter, approached the LEA with a view to securing a financial contribution towards the cost of this, having first established that the existing PPS, set up with GEST funding, was at that time barely operational. Discussions with the LEA convinced them of the potential of the organisation to provide an independent quality framework in which to offer parental support across Essex.

Essex is a large county with 12 district councils and one county council. The ethnic minority population is only 1.8 per cent. In January 2000 there were 4,429 children with statements of SEN. There were 215 permanent exclusions in 1998–99 out of a school population of 194,108 pupils. The LEA is committed to a policy of inclusion which it recognises can only be achieved over a number of years.

Families InFocus (Essex) has endeavoured to respond to requests for assistance from parents in Mid-Essex at whatever stage of assessment and statementing their child is at. Resources for this initially came from the National Lottery and joint finance. Responding to demands from both parents and professionals, in 1999 the charity embarked on a programme to offer its services countywide at the same time as the government was introducing funding for PPS through the Standards Fund. The LEA decided to provide the bulk of the PPS itself and restricted the funding allocated to Families InFocus (Essex) to the provision of support at Stage 4 and above. With its commitment to providing a service countywide at other stages of the Code of Practice, the organisation has sought funding from other sources.

When new money became available to enhance the PPS scheme, the LEA used this to address its new responsibilities and increase its staffing levels. A number of attempts on the part of Families InFocus (Essex) were made to engage parents in a discussion on the strategic direction of the PPS scheme. It became apparent that the values aspired to by Families InFocus (Essex) in terms of empowerment and involving users in decision-making were not immediately compatible with those of the LEA officers.

The reality, as acknowledged by all concerned, is that the resourcing of an IPS scheme, which is available to any family going through the assessment and statementing process, is a major challenge due to the large numbers involved. In early discussions with the LEA they indicated that they wished to control the system of referrals to us. Initial concerns that families therefore would not gain access to the service were soon overtaken by events as satisfied users told other parents about the IPS scheme. We continue to believe that the best possible outcomes are likely to be obtained and emotions and resources saved when families access the IPS service as early as possible. Our intervention enables parents to start to address their own emotional distress, which may be the barrier to effective communication with the school.

Independence and partnership

Committed to its core values of empowerment and supporting families to access services and obtain their rights, we have jealously guarded our independence. The organisation owes its existence to the views of parents expressed at the time of the initial multi-agency research and subsequently. Although professionals may have the skills and the commitment to providing an excellent service, the pain and very deep emotions that families experience when dealing with their child's needs can only be addressed in an environment where they will not be judged and their own needs for support will be addressed. People faced with difficult decisions, which may have lifelong implications, routinely seek a second opinion or look for a sounding board to help them come to terms with the issues facing them.

There is some debate as to whether IPS schemes need to be totally independent of their LEAs or whether the issue is more of impartiality or neutrality. We are yet to be convinced that neutral and impartial support can be given by any LEA in the context of legislative requirements for inclusion. This is a widespread issue referred to later in this chapter. The nature of the independence relates primarily to the governance and resourcing of the scheme rather than to working in isolation from the professionals in the statutory services. Clearly the latter is not an option if the interests of the child are to be paramount in accordance with the Children Act 1989.

Issues of independence and impartiality are very real for parents who may perceive the funding as being conditional on the scheme buying into an overtly inclusive policy which is contrary to their own wishes or who may feel that they will be pushed into complying with the LEA's or the school's views about how best to meet their child's needs in the context of limited resources. Some parents have an entrenched distrust of schools and the LEA based on their own negative experiences and unresolved emotional problems associated with their child's diagnosis.

They also are wary of the implications for confidentiality. Families InFocus (Essex) has found difficulty with the type of monitoring information requested by the LEA which could lead to individual families being identified. However often we enable a family to explore the options available to them and assure them that should the situation arise and our funding were threatened, we would continue to provide the service albeit by seeking alternative sources of finance, there are still those who perceive us as being in the pocket of the LEA. A parent we approached as part of a user survey said that, although she was happy with the support she had received, she did not wish to take part in the survey, as she understood the LEA was a key funder: 'I am unsure as to Essex LEA's role with regards to "Independent", confidentiality/anonymity and parental views!'

Issues of independence are recognised in the National Parent Partnership Network (2001) *Information Exchange: 12 July 2001*. They are more significant with regard to support concerning SEN Appeal Tribunals. An IPS scheme operated by an LEA cannot provide any realistic help at this stage because its workers are legally part of the agency the family is appealing against! The support for parents in preparation for Tribunals is an increasing part of our work.

The nature of partnership is the subject of other debates as local authorities merge with health services. Perceptions of it depend on organisational cultures, individual experiences (e.g. marriage, business), and so on. They can vary from, at one end of the spectrum, one partner acting as agent of the other to carry out their work and at the other end of the spectrum to both partners being involved in all decisions and taking equal responsibility for those decisions. In essence, this is all about a difference in power balances. Despite changes which give more rights and responsibilities to parents, there still are those who perceive the culture of the education system as one where the teacher is the figure of authority, the repository of knowledge and the keeper of discipline. This makes it very difficult for many parents to feel that they have any power at all over their child's destiny in the school environment.

If parents are to be true partners in the education of their children, a frank and honest exchange of views must be facilitated and this can only happen if there is recognition of the inherent power structures. As one foster carer has said to us, 'I am not going to tell the school about my family circumstances and the difficulties we are having because they will abuse the confidence and use the information against me.'

Most parents, even those who do not attend school meetings, feel strongly about their child's education but emotions often get in the way of reason. Those who are well educated or who are teachers find handling situations where they have to emphasise the negative aspects of their child in order to obtain the resources for their child's education, very distressing. As one teacher who worked in a pupil referral unit said, 'I thought with all my experience of handling difficult children and their parents I could cope with my own child. But it is *very* different when you are at the receiving end!'

Acknowledgement of the passion that a parent brings to any scenario involving their child with SEN can be the foundation on which to build a positive relationship. The passion can be apparent in both mother and father. Often fathers will distance themselves from the everyday events mothers have to take on board in caring for their child but when it comes to educational issues they become more visible. For many fathers this may be the first time they have had an opportunity to voice their concerns about their child's impairment or difficulties and feel able to do something positive to try to mitigate the effects of an impairment. The result is that those at the receiving end get the full force of the pent-up anger, pain and guilt which have been accumulating since the child's diagnosis and which may never have been articulated before. Frequently parents tell us that they have lived for years with their child's difficulties and have never been able to speak to anybody, even their partner, about how they feel.

An holistic service

Families InFocus (Essex) was set up with a specific remit to address the emotional needs of parents and carers of children with disabilities and special needs. In addition to the Independent Parental Supporter scheme we provide the following:

- one-stop specialist signposting information helpline;
- parent-to-parent befriending service;
- family support work including advice and assistance to gain access to existing services, help with Disability Living Allowance claims and appeals;
- drop-in facilities;
- play and crèche facilities;
- fun activities for siblings;
- counselling;
- group activities for families – social events, workshops, etc.;
- participation in planning and consultation with statutory bodies.

Integral to all these services is the ability to address the emotional needs of parents and carers. This has influenced the development of the IPS scheme in that volunteers are all expected to have parenting experience but not necessarily of a child with SEN.

Core values

The fundamental principles which underpin all our work are the following:

1. Do no damage to users.
2. Respect the views of parents and enable them to fulfil their responsibilities subject to there being:
   (a) no risk to themselves or others and in particular to their children;
   (b) no criminal act committed.
3. Maintain confidentiality subject to 2 above.
4. Empower users to gain and retain control over their lives.
5. Enable them to access existing services.
6. Observe good equal opportunities, anti-oppressive and anti-discriminatory practice.
7. Enable the views of parents to be expressed and communicated to the decision-makers in the process of planning and delivery of services.
8. Work in partnership with other agencies where appropriate to promote the health and well-being of parents/carers, thereby ensuring that the health and well-being of the whole family are promoted.
9. Where the needs of the child conflict with those of the parent, the child's needs are paramount.

Parental input

From the outset it was decided to involve parents in the guidance of the IPS scheme. To this end they were encouraged to join the Advisory Group whose terms of reference are the following:

1. Ensure the independence of the IPS scheme.
2. Enable parents of children with SEN in Essex to raise and consider issues of interest and concern particularly in relationship to their child's assessment and/or statementing of SEN.
3. Undertake investigations into relevant matters and where appropriate to make recommendations.
4. Encourage the continuous raising of standards in the provision of independent parental support.
5. Monitor progress of the scheme and assist in its promotion.
6. Facilitate consultation with parents of children with SEN.
7. Encourage anti-discriminatory and anti-oppressive practice and ensure that the scheme is accessible to all sections of the community.

Human resources and training

With limited resources available for setting up a service to cover a county as large and varied in its composition as Essex, and with no certainty of ongoing funding, in true voluntary sector fashion, a flexible structure was devised. Recognising the potential of the IPS scheme to make a difference to the education and lives of many thousands of children in Essex (approximately 28,000 across all stages of assessment and statementing) a coordinator/trainer, Janet Hill, was appointed. Janet had many years of experience training for the Pre-School Learning Alliance with a particular focus on special needs and was coordinator of our parent-to-parent befriending scheme.

In recruiting volunteers, we are committed to promoting good equal opportunities practice. However, we are still struggling to reconcile this with the need for them to have the requisite literacy, communication and mobility skills to enable them to visit any family in their home without presenting the family with additional obstacles to achieving their aims as smoothly as possible. The complexity of the statutory forms demands at the very least a basic education. The timing of meetings invariably requires that the IPS be available during school hours. This limits the pool of potential volunteers, which in itself is dwindling due to demographic changes, full employment and the childcare revolution, which attracts women back into paid work.

Key attributes for an Independent Parental Supporter are:

1. Daytime availability – this will continue to be necessary while schools persist in scheduling meetings at times which meet their rather than the family's needs.
2. Competence to deal with written materials.
3. Parenting experience – not necessarily of a child with SEN but so they can relate to the passion parents bring to the issues they are dealing with and to give them an immediate source of empathy.
4. Car owner – depending on proximity to schools and realistic alternative forms of transport.
5. Attendance at support groups – there is no automatic right for an IPS to continue if s/he has missed two of these in a row. In these circumstances his/her currency and availability are reviewed.

Attendance at the course does not necessarily confer a right to becoming an IPS.

Key tasks and responsibilities of an IPS are to do the following:

1. Listen to the family and respect their views.
2. Assist in the completion of paperwork, answering correspondence, etc. and provide appropriate assistance in the assessment and statementing of the child's special educational needs.

3. Accompany the family to meetings, reviews, appeals, etc.
4. Facilitate communication between the family and relevant agencies.
5. Attend support meetings and ongoing training.
6. Keep appropriate records.
7. Raise any issues of concern with the IPS coordinator and inform the Director of Families InFocus (Essex) of any child protection concerns.
8. Observe confidentiality within the IPS guidelines.
9. Be prepared to have a conscientious and flexible approach, e.g. meeting deadlines, keeping appointments, responding quickly to a request for support.
10. Read and comply with all Families InFocus (Essex) policies, including health and safety, equal opportunities and confidentiality.

The training course built on the good practice of our existing volunteer befriending scheme and identified the expectations of parents. The rolling programme takes place in various venues around the county to make them as accessible as possible. Carried out in term time during school hours, the course starts with an introductory session designed to encourage interested people to come along to find out more without being obliged to sign up.

The sessions cover the following:

- confidentiality, disability awareness, equal opportunities, SEN, child protection;
- SEN Code of Practice – national and local framework, inclusion;
- listening skills;
- working with professionals and parents as partners;
- stages of assessment, Individual Education Plans;
- Statements;
- Annual Reviews, SEN Tribunal, 14+ and transitions;
- assertiveness, negotiation skills, conflict resolution and empowerment;
- practical issues, health and safety, complaints, evaluation.

We recognise that however independent an organisation may be, at the end of the day, the child has to go to school. We therefore ensure that 'the other side's' views are represented in the training courses. Staff from the LEA, including educational psychologists, administrators and Special Educational Needs Coordinators (SENCOs), contribute to sessions. They too have gained by listening to parents' views in an environment of cooperation and mutual respect.

Key worker

As the scheme evolved, we recognised the need for a key worker to support individual families. The type of support required varied from complex issues at Appeal Tribunal level to basic form filling and attendance at relatively uncontentious school meetings. We also recognised the potential for litigation against Families InFocus (Essex) if we got it wrong, particularly in light of the fervour with which many parents pursue their cause.

This has led us to identify at the outset the issues, complexity and appropriate key worker to deal with the referral whether a volunteer or paid member of staff. Complicated issues, those pertaining to exclusions or appeals, are dealt with by the Deputy Director or the coordinator. While several volunteers are developing their expertise and confidence as they deal with more cases, the trustees have made a policy decision that volunteers should not be given these potentially litigious cases. The level of control that an organisation has over a volunteer is limited but the damage they could cause both in terms of the way they work with families and to the reputation of the organisation is substantial. The remedies for Families InFocus (Essex) would, in contrast, be negligible.

The robust vetting and support structure for volunteers that has been built into the system partially mitigates the inherent risks. Trainees on the courses are not accepted as accredited volunteers by Families InFocus (Essex) until they have satisfactorily completed 80 per cent of the course. The last session enables participants to discuss and assess each other alongside the assessment made by the coordinator/trainer. Recognising that a significant proportion of the trainees are parents of children with SEN, we are concerned to ensure that IPSs are both emotionally and practically available to undertake the work without dumping their own issues on the users. In addition to the police checks carried out on our behalf by the LEA, we follow up two references for each IPS.

IPSs keep in close contact with the coordinator/trainer with their first cases and they receive individual supervision. Group support meetings are convened termly where issues rather than individual families are discussed, thereby providing an ongoing learning opportunity for the IPSs. Twice yearly top-up training is provided to ensure currency and address new topics or to cover issues more comprehensively (e.g. child protection and courses of action to be taken).

Links with other bodies

We have actively sought representatives from other voluntary organisations to train as IPSs as we recognise their local and often specialist knowledge about specific conditions. This has led to difficulties in supervising and monitoring their activities as their relationships with their own client group sometimes prohibit the sharing of information. In these situations IPSs are required to sign a disclaimer absolving Families InFocus (Essex) of any liability.

Families InFocus (Essex) has strong links with the Advisory Centre for Education through its accredited use of their Step by Step advisers' handbooks. Their training has been used both for staff and volunteers and their advisers' helpline has proved a useful source for a second opinion. The National Council for Disabled Children was particularly supportive in our early days. The Director of Families InFocus (Essex) has also valued the links established through her membership of the NASEN Parent Partnership Standing Group. We have also taken advantage on several occasions of the proximity of the Children's Legal Centre based at Essex University for free legal advice for families.

Working in tandem with the LEA

Although we are independent, we have welcomed opportunities to work closely with the LEA where appropriate. As previously mentioned, LEA staff have made significant contributions to the training of the IPSs, thereby ensuring that they are able to appreciate the differing responsibilities and perspectives of all the players in the assessment process. The Director of Families InFocus (Essex) was involved in the interviewing of the Parent Partnership Coordinator employed by the LEA.

In the early days, several schools were not very receptive to our role as advocates and supporters of certain families whom they perceived as confrontational. A key educational psychologist enabled some of these situations to be turned around very quickly into one of cooperation by advising the school about the benefits of our participation.

At the end of each course, new IPSs visit the local SEN and Psychology Service office to meet the staff they are most likely to be dealing with.

We have plans to amend our funding agreement and clarify the data to be collected.

Empowerment and rights

Fundamental to our work are the rights of the child as set out in the UN Convention on the Rights of the Child and the notion of empowerment. Due to the potential volume of work and a respect for individuals, Families InFocus (Essex) has striven to prevent a dependency culture developing among its users.

Families InFocus (Essex) has been privileged to support many families through some very distressing situations and help them to move on in their lives. Support for families regarding exclusions, both temporary and permanent, has become a regular feature of our work.

As an agent for change we have seen many positive outcomes not only with regard to the child's needs but also those of other family members. To cite a few examples: the parent with poor educational attainment and dyslexia who attended evening classes to improve her literacy skills; the parents whose child had ADHD who were able to give up smoking; the father whose history of violence necessitated him being accompanied to a school meeting by a police officer and who found ways of handling his own anger as a result of the ground rules imposed as a condition of our IPS involvement.

Our experience has reinforced our belief in the importance of an independent structure being made available to parents who want it. Two examples illustrate this:

- The parents whose child was repeatedly being excluded from school on a temporary basis were being threatened by the educational welfare officer with being taken to court for the child's non-attendance.
- The family referred by the Child and Family Consultation Service where the child had been permanently excluded from school and the family had been left in limbo because none of the educational professionals appeared to wish to take responsibility for initiating any alternative form of education for the child.

Both these families had satisfactory outcomes as a result of our participation.

Future plans

We are looking at ways of improving accessibility to the scheme through additional drop-in sessions around the county, periodic roadshows and leafleting to all schools, both mainstream and special. Accreditation of the training would recognise the valuable contribution of the volunteer IPSs.

Families InFocus (Essex)'s practice may also change in the light of the revised Code of Practice and new legislation. The evolving relationship with the LEA and continually improved dialogue with them enable past teething problems to be put to one side.

As an organisation working primarily to support parents and carers, we have identified a need for separate representation of the child's views especially when these are at odds with those of the parents. We anticipate that work we are just beginning alongside Colchester MIND in relation to adolescent mental health advocacy will grow.

Indications are that early intervention may prevent further distress and problems. Our independence and non-judgemental approach appear to enable families to confront their emotional needs and face up to issues which may hitherto have proved obstacles to progress and productive relationships with schools and the LEA.

Legislation (e.g. the Human Rights Act) raises people's expectations and willingness to seek redress for perceived injustices. If this trend continues, there will be more pressure on IPS schemes to employ staff whose actions are more easily monitored and controlled. As demographic and economic changes absorb the pool of potential volunteers, paying staff may be the only viable way to provide the service.

Conclusion

With a rights-based approach tempered with compassion and acknowledgement that parents only want the best for their child, families' own unresolved emotional issues can be addressed rather than getting in the way of meaningful dialogue and productive relationships with professionals. The Families InFocus (Essex) model for an IPS scheme enables the emotions which drive parents to continue what they call 'the fight' for a better deal for their child in an unequal society to be harnessed positively for the long-term benefit of the whole family. In contrast, the role of the educators is sometimes seen as limited to short-term solutions for the benefit of the child only.

Finally, these quotations from satisfied parents summarise the *raison d'être* of an IPS scheme which operates independently of the LEA but alongside it:

> Without the involvement of an IPS we would have given up. She provided the support and encouragement for us to continue.

> I would not have known what my next step was without my IPS. He was so friendly and helpful.

Reference

National Parent Partnership Network (2001) *Information Exchange: 12 July 2001*. London: Council for Disabled Children, National Children's Bureau.

Chapter 10

Pioneering Parent Partnership Services in Wales: the SNAP Cymru experience

Roger Bishop

Introduction

In this chapter I trace the parent-led development of the Parent Partnership work of SNAP Cymru from its origins in the mid-1980s to the present; identifying the services it provides and looking forward to the challenges provided by legislation and a new SEN Code of Practice.

Origins

Like many voluntary organisations the Special Needs Advisory Project, SNAP Cymru, was started by a group of visionary people responding to an urgent need which was for parents of children with special educational needs to find their way through the maze of bureaucracy to the provision they felt their children needed. The time was the mid-1980s – a time for optimism, idealism and innovation in services for people with learning difficulties in Wales. The All Wales Mental Handicap Strategy (AWS) (Welsh Office 1983) had created a new climate through a powerful statement of principles and, crucially, additional funding. Its aim was to create opportunities and services that would support people with learning disabilities in the community and remove reliance upon institutional and segregated forms of service.

Although the AWS made only passing reference to education, it echoed Section two of the 1981 Education Act seeking 'the maximum possible access and integration with ordinary education facilities' (p. 7). It is also important to note that the AWS envisaged a multidisciplinary, multi-agency approach, which involved the participation of people with learning disabilities as well as their parents and carers.

Following the Warnock Report (DES 1978), the Education Act 1981 also gave parents of children with special educational needs (SEN) new rights and responsibilities, enabling them to be fully involved in their children's assessment and to express their preference for the type of education they should receive. In practice, however, many parents continued to find the experience of wresting some control over their children's education to be deeply frustrating and stressful.

These, then, were the elements that combined to create Parent Partnership work in Wales through the development of SNAP Cymru: parental expectations of a brighter future for their children fuelled by Warnock, the 1981 Education Act and the All Wales Strategy set against bureaucracy and professional attitudes and practices that were sometimes slow to change.

Practicalities

If the Special Needs Advisory Project can be said to have a moment of conception, that moment was a one day conference held at Swansea University on Saturday 19th April 1986.

(Roberts 1989: i)

The aim of the conference, organised by Mencap in Wales was 'to provide an understanding of the 1981 Education Act which will enable parents to fully participate with the Education Authorities in the best choice of education provision for their child'. Speakers, including Sheila Wolfendale, editor of this book, addressed parents as well as delegates from statutory and voluntary organisations. Following the conference, in June 1986, a meeting of Mid Glamorgan parents began to define the service they wanted and set out the original aims and objectives of SNAP Cymru. Up to this point Mencap in Wales, the Spastics Society (now Scope) and Wales Council for the Disabled had attempted to provide advice and support services for families who had contacted them. Now the vision of a unified support service to families began to emerge.

The original aims of this new organisation were:

to reach as many parents of children with special educational needs as possible, to help them in their understanding of the philosophy of the 1981 Education Act. It will encourage parents to participate in the education of their children and contribute fully and equally with the professionals in the identification of suitable provision for their children.

In its first leaflet to families SNAP offered to do the following:

- Explain your rights under the 1981 Education Act.
- Provide information about schools in your area.

- Help you in your discussions with professionals.
- Help you describe your child's needs.
- Perhaps introduce you to parents who have similar difficulties.

Initially, the SNAP Cymru service was delivered by staff from Mencap and Scope who set about training a group of volunteers who would, in some ways, carry out the role of 'Named Person' envisaged by the Warnock Report, but omitted from the 1981 Education Act.

In 1987 SNAP received a grant from the 'Opportunities for Volunteering' fund to establish a pilot project in the counties of Mid Glamorgan, West Glamorgan and Gwent. The project was officially launched in 1988 and received 183 referrals in its pilot year. Subsequent years saw successful bids being made for funding to establish SNAP Cymru services in counties across Wales. The funding obtained reflected SNAP Cymru's contention that support for families of children with SEN is the combined business of Education, Health and Social Services. The Mid Glamorgan project was funded in 1989 through the 'Joint Finance of Community Care Projects'. All Wales Strategy funding subsequently enabled the service to develop in Mid Glamorgan, South Glamorgan, Gwent and Dyfed. This level of expansion put considerable pressure on Mencap in Wales and the Spastics Society (now Scope) for resources and central coordination and so SNAP Cymru was established as an independent charity in 1993 with the help of 'core funding' from the Welsh Office.

The publishing of the SEN Code of Practice in 1994 gave the organisation further impetus as many local authorities and parents looked to SNAP Cymru to provide the 'Named Person' that Warnock had recommended 14 years earlier. By the year ending April 2001, 12 years after the pilot phase, SNAP Cymru was providing a service to families from every one of the 22 unitary Welsh local authorities and receiving funding from 18 of those authorities. The remaining four counties that had made up the former Clwyd authority contracted with the Citizens Advice Bureau to provide Named Person services.

A comparison of the recorded referrals from 1989–2000, 1999–2000 and 2000–01 gives an indication of the scale of growth in demand for the information, support and advice that SNAP Cymru provides, and is shown in Table 10.1.

Other data indicates that in 1989–90 SNAP Cymru was mainly supporting families of children with learning disabilities and physical disabilities with 68 per cent and 17 per cent of the referrals respectively (reflecting the Mencap and Scope influence in the organisation). However, by 1999–2000 the proportion of referrals from these groups had fallen to 17 per cent and 5 per cent respectively (although the overall numbers were increasing). Other changes over the period have been:

Table 10.1 Number of referrals by county

County*	1989–90	1999–00	2000–01
Bridgend		120	162
Caerphilly		113	127
Merthyr		24	42
Rhondda, Cynon, Taff		101	145
Total Mid Glam	120	358	476
Cardiff		391	482
Vale of Glam		93	100
Total South Glam	18	489	582
Blaenau Gwent		27	38
Monmouthshire		48	31
Newport		97	123
Torfaen		74	77
Total Gwent	90	246	269
Gwynedd		219	204
Ynys Mon/Anglesey		117	71
Denbighshire[†]		4	5
Conwy[†]		24	43
Flintshire[†]		12	6
Wrexham[†]		6	1
Total North Wales	0	382	330
Ceredigion		78	50
Powys		46	94
Total Mid Wales	0	124	144
Pembrokeshire	0	94	142
Swansea		248	245
Neath/Port Talbot		208	206
Total West Glam	125	456	451
Carmarthenshire	0	72	72
Outside Wales	0	13	11
Total	353	2251	2477

*In 1989–90 there were eight counties in Wales. In 1996 local government reorganisation created 22 unitary authorities to replace them.
[†]CAB provide a Named Person service in these counties.

- emotional and behavioural difficulties rising from 6 per cent to 17 per cent;
- specific learning difficulties rising from 5 per cent to 21 per cent;
- sensory impairment rising marginally from 3 per cent to 4 per cent.

Another feature has been the increased support to families of children at risk of exclusion from school – approximately 5 per cent of referrals in 2000–01.

In 2000–01 76 per cent of all referrals were male and 24 per cent female. Age at referral is shown in Figure 10.1.

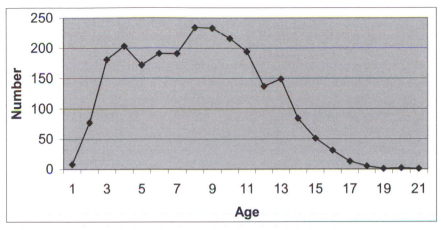

Figure 10.1 Age at referral to SNAP Cymru 2000–01

How does SNAP Cymru work?

The organisation's current mission statement sets the scene:

> SNAP Cymru will enable families (parents, carers, children and young people) to have their voices heard within decision-making processes of special educational needs, and supports them to influence policy and practice in the planning and delivery of services.

SNAP Cymru sees its role as one of promoting and encouraging partnership between families and professionals in SEN planning and decision-making processes.

In order to make the sometimes problematic (Vernon 1999: 8) concept of working in partnership more tangible, SNAP Cymru developed a Partnership Charter (SNAP Cymru 1998) in consultation with LEAs and parents and launched it at its all Wales Conference in 1998. The principles of the Charter reflect the organisation's overall approach and form the basis for service level agreements with partner agencies.

How is SNAP Cymru organised?

SNAP Cymru currently employs 34 full- and part-time staff. As Director I am accountable to a board of trustees made up of parents, voluntary organisation representatives and people with specific expertise, e.g. a university lecturer with an expertise in SEN, a manager of a multi-disciplinary team supporting children with disabilities and their families. I manage a head office team responsible for strategy, training, quality assurance, fundraising, finance, outreach services and operational management of the seven branches across Wales. Each branch team is led by a Branch Manager responsible for the development of the service within the branch area including the recruitment, training and management of volunteers.

Wolfendale and Cook (1997) and Vernon (1999) identify similar core activities undertaken by voluntary sector Parent Partnership Services in England:

- the provision of advice and support to parents on an individual basis either person to person, in clinics or surgeries or by telephone;
- the dissemination of information to parents;
- the provision of training;
- the setting up and running of parent support groups.

(Vernon 1999)

Although its main service has been the provision of information, support and advice, SNAP Cymru has, to an extent, engaged in all of these activities as well as the development of SEN policy and practice at local and national level. It gains great strength from the following features:

- *It is driven by parents.* Research emphasises the importance of parent perspectives to effective partnership working in SEN (Vernon 1999). Across Wales at local level SNAP Cymru Branch Advisory Groups gather parental views, link parents and professionals, and provide opportunities for consultation on SEN policy and procedure.
- *It is independent of the local authority.* As an independent charity SNAP Cymru is able to offer impartial information, support and advice to families of children with SEN. There are times when its independence is perceived to be under threat from the service level agreements it has with LEAs who part pay for the service through National Assembly GEST funding. However, the nature of this relationship can also have the advantage of ensuring a dialogue that can lead to improved partnership working, for example, collaboration on written information to families about the SEN process has occurred in a number of counties (cf. Torfaen Education Department 1997). SNAP Cymru then is sufficiently independent of the LEA to be impartial but in a close enough relationship to contribute to its policy and practice.
- *One organisation covers many LEA areas.* This provides the opportunity to develop a consistent quality of service based on common objectives and quality standards as well as benefit from the cross-fertilisation of ideas which a network of local branches generates.

It can be argued that the main inconsistency across Wales is one of service levels rather that service quality. There is a wide variation in the level of investment, which the 22 Welsh LEAs have made in the provision of IPS/Named Person Services. Monies allocated for this purpose from LEA GEST funds ranged from zero to £25,000 in 2000–01. While the National Assembly for Wales has echoed the commitment to Parent Partnership expressed in the DfEE document *Meeting Special Educational Needs: A Programme of Action* (1998), in its parallel document *Shaping the Future for Special Education: An Action Programme for Wales* (Welsh Office 1999), funding has been more illusory. There have been no ring-fenced monies to implement the policy to compare with the £18 million over three years included in the Standards Fund in England. SNAP Cymru has been able to continue to develop, despite comparatively low levels of LEA investment, because of its ability to add value by drawing in funding from social services, health and grant giving bodies.

Current challenges

Disagreement resolution/mediation

Urey and Fisher (1988) suggest that resolving disagreements around people's *interests* is generally far more productive than resolution based on *rights* or on the basis of *power*. This seems to uphold the view that partnership work, developing a relationship of trust between families and professionals, can prevent future conflict, which in some instances, may result in an appeal to the arbitration of the Special Educational Needs Tribunal. SNAP Cymru provides support at any point along the continuum in Figure 10.2 up to and including the appeal itself.

We consider that it is important to provide information, advice and support as soon as possible after parents identify that their child may have special educational needs. Consequently, in some counties SNAP Cymru has established Early Years services to families as part of Sure Start-funded multi-agency initiatives.

Independent Parental Supporters can often mediate informally between the school or LEA and parents. In practice, this often leads

Figure 10.2 The disagreement resolution continuum

to a satisfactory resolution of a disagreement before an appeal reaches the SEN Tribunal. In order to improve its capability to intervene in disagreements in this way SNAP Cymru has started an in-service programme of mediation training to run alongside its Open College-accredited induction course for staff and volunteers.

To complement local services SNAP Cymru has also recruited a group of independent trained accredited mediators, who can provide formal mediation, in an attempt to resolve disagreements before the SEN Tribunal hears an appeal. The Special Educational Needs and Disability Act 2001 and the new SEN Code of Practice both place a duty on LEAs to use disagreement resolution arrangements in order to avoid unnecessary recourse to arbitration at the SEN Tribunal, which can be an adversarial process.

Hall (1999: 5) described the process of mediation and identified several models of mediation being used in English Parent Partnership Schemes. Her report endorsed an approach broadly in line with the service designed by SNAP Cymru - emphasising the usefulness of LEAs contracting with independent organisations such as SNAP.

> An independent organisation is able to provide a truly independent service and one that can be tailored to meet and be driven by local needs. Other advantages include objectivity; credibility; the ability to empower parents so that they can make informed choices; the quality and type of advice that is provided; and the ability to provide access to additional help in the form of putting people in touch with support groups and networks of local parents.
>
> (Ibid.: 14)

SNAP Cymru's mediation service for Gloucestershire PPS is an example of how this can work in practice. The service level agreement (Gloucestershire LEA and SNAP Cymru 2000) describes the purpose of the service:

> To provide recognised and accredited mediation/conciliation skills to Gloucestershire Local Education Authority (LEA) so that it can offer an independent mediation/conciliation service to parents of children with special educational needs.
>
> When will the service operate?
> - When an appeal has been lodged with the Special Educational Needs Tribunal (SENT).
> - When a disagreement has occurred that may lead to an appeal.
>
> Expected outcomes.
> - A negotiated agreement.
> - Both parties feel that all avenues to a possible agreement have been fully explored.
> - Parents feel that further action on their part has not been unjustifiably delayed or altered.

SNAP Cymru has found it effective to team a member of staff who has also undertaken mediation training with an independent mediator, thus combining SEN expertise with mediation skills. Although the service is in its infancy we believe that it will in some circumstances help resolve disagreements and reduce dependency on the SEN Tribunal.

Piloting school-based SNAP Cymru Services

> In the past the only time I have talked to the teacher is when they ring because John is in trouble again. It was nice to talk to a teacher without feeling guilty and defensive.
>
> (Parent)

Although the substantial rise in referrals to SNAP Cymru's service (detailed above) means that more families in Wales are receiving Parent Partnership Services than ever before, there are clearly considerable challenges in facilitating an even wider access to the information, advice and support of Independent Parental Supporters (IPS) for all families of children with SEN from a national population of 2.8 million people. As Vernon points out:

> Schools have a unique contribution to make to partnership with parents: not only are they obliged to work with parents, they are ideally placed to ensure that the dialogue between parents and professional is established at an early stage of assessing and identifying a child's special educational needs.
>
> (1999: 62)

In recent years SNAP Cymru has begun to facilitate school-based partnership services in order to improve accessibility to the support and information families need. Pilot schemes have been developed in primary and comprehensive schools as well as work in a pupil referral unit in Swansea. A project in a primary school in Carmarthenshire set the following objectives in February 2000.

- Establish links with School Link Advisor, Head, SENCO, School Governors and support teachers to explore ways of providing a SNAP Cymru service to families of children with SEN at all stages of the SEN Code of Practice.
- Look at present information on SEN to parents. Devise ways in line with new legislation and the new draft Code of Practice, in which the school may become the initial and main provider of information to families.
- Design and distribute school/parent information to families and SNAP Cymru leaflets to families.

- Organise family information days within the school and community.
- Establish regular school or community SNAP Cymru surgeries.
- Promote the SNAP Cymru service within the community via local networks and media.
- Recruit and train Independent Parental Supporters within the school and community.

There have been positive outcomes in these projects in terms of improved information and communication between parents and professionals. Meetings and events have been organised which have included parents, health visitors, social services, employment services, police, youth offending teams, careers, LEA, children and youth partnerships, Sure Start and the voluntary sector.

However, other objectives have been more difficult to achieve. Surgeries in schools have proved difficult to establish and the notion of locating IPS in the school has also proved problematical, as parents seem to prefer to speak to an IPS outside the school environment. An alternative approach under consideration is the notion of an IPS link person based in the school who can provide basic information and refer on to an IPS caseworker.

Support of looked after children and their carers

There are over 3,000 children and young people in public care in Wales, many of whom have special educational needs. The obstacles they have to face in reaching their educational potential (Jackson 2001) is at last being recognised in public policy (DfEE/DH 2000).

The following case study illustrates the impact that timely Parent Partnership work can have in assisting local authorities with their corporate parenting role.

Case study A

Rhys (not his real name) is seven and lives with long-term foster parents. He has moderate to severe learning difficulties and a severe receptive and expressive language disorder. The LEA considered that his needs would be best met in a special school for children with severe learning difficulties and a proposed statement of needs recommended this. However, Rhys' foster family felt that he had settled well into his local primary school and wanted him to continue there. The social worker assigned to the family had no knowledge of educational issues and contacted SNAP Cymru for help.

The SNAP Cymru IPS was able explain the SEN process to the family and social worker. She arranged a meeting with the school to discuss how Rhys' needs could be met. When enough evidence had been gathered, from the family, social services, the school and therapists, SNAP arranged a meeting with the LEA who agreed that he could stay at his local mainstream primary with 15 hours per week non-teaching support. SNAP Cymru was also able to signpost the family to local support groups and play sessions for children with special educational needs.

Rhys has just had a glowing annual review. All his physio-therapy, occupational therapy and speech and language therapy now take place at the school.

The family think that at some time in the future he may have to move to a more specialist provision. 'At the moment he is doing well, he is slower than his peers but has made many friends with children from the local community and he is accepted.' The foster family is very pleased that they sought advice and feel that it has resulted in a better quality of life for Rhys.

Care coordination/key working

SNAP Cymru has found that in carrying out the Named Person/IPS role it is often in the position of being *de facto* the key worker for families with support needs, which go beyond the child's educational needs. As a result, SNAP staff and volunteers often find themselves helping families with Disability Living Allowance forms or applying for services such as respite care.

The effective multi-agency coordination of services for children with disabilities, while an apparently straightforward concept, has often proved difficult to implement across organisational boundaries. There is, however, research available on the effective implementation of key working (Mukherjee *et al.* 1999), a comprehensive form of service coordination, which provides families with emotional support, information and advocacy. SNAP Cymru is one of a number of agencies involved in a key-working scheme currently being set up in Pembrokeshire.

For a number of children there are workers involved who are undertaking some of the key worker roles and it may be more appropriate for these workers to continue as the identified co-ordination key worker, e.g. workers within voluntary organisations like SNAP Cymru and SCOPE, and social workers and community nurses with disabled children on their caseloads.

(Pembrokeshire Children's Centre 2000)

The following is an example of how the IPS role can develop into a key worker role for the benefit of both child and family.

Case Study B

SNAP Cymru has been working with a family of four children, two of whom have special educational needs. Following the annual review of the elder child who has mental health needs, SNAP requested a planning meeting with Social Services and a health review. Prior to the planning meeting with Social Services, the SNAP worker helped the family write down all their concerns and subsequently assisted in the drawing up of the care plan. The health review required an appointment 100 miles away in Cardiff. The SNAP worker applied to a trust fund and the family received £150 to help with the expense of travel to see the specialist. The child now has a health plan and a care plan. The SNAP worker is attempting to ensure that in future these separate planning processes are integrated as part the key-working scheme.

Parent partnership or family partnership?

SNAP Cymru recognises the need for young people to receive independent information, support and advice. With the help of a grant from BBC Children in Need the organisation is developing a 'family partnership approach' – extending its capacity to deliver its services direct to young people. The first phase, recently ended, has seen the development of policies and training that will enable SNAP and partner agencies to improve the involvement of young people in discussions about their special educational needs. The second phase aims to develop children's advocacy and a direct referral service for young people with SEN.

Evaluation of effectiveness

SNAP Cymru has grown significantly in recent years and consequently has needed to upgrade its systems. It is, therefore, endeavouring to ensure best value through its use of the Charities Evaluation Service's 'PQASSO' Quality Assurance System (1998) and its successful pursuit of the Community Legal Service Quality Mark (Legal Services

Commission 2000). It is also vital that the organisation knows in what ways partner agencies and families feel it can improve its services and to this end it has undertaken consumer satisfaction surveys. From these and the analysis of our statistics, we know that wider access to the service, particularly from socially excluded groups, is one of our main challenges. Although SNAP does not operate a waiting list, families may sometimes experience a delay because of the constant demand for the service. We may need to consider how we limit the length of casework by developing a more robust case closure policy.

SNAP Cymru is also aware of a lower than expected take-up of the service from ethnic minority communities and people whose first language is Welsh. We are taking steps to increase the number of staff and volunteers who can operate in the medium of Welsh and minority languages with the help of a grant from the Community Fund.

At the time of writing, an evaluation of Parent Partnership work in Wales is being undertaken by Sheila Wolfendale and Trevor Bryans, funded by the National Association for Special Educational Needs and the National Assembly for Wales. SNAP Cymru is keen to use the outcomes of the evaluation to further improve and develop the accessibility, quality and range of its services (contact author for details: see Sources, p. 142).

Future directions

SNAP Cymru is unusual as a Parent Partnership Service whose policy and strategic direction are led by families rather than local authorities. It is probably now the largest corporate provider of Parent Partnership Services in England and Wales. However, the challenges of legislation and the new SEN Code of Practice will provide opportunities for collaboration (and the possibility of competition) with other like-minded organisations. (Examples of recent collaboration include the visual impairment training provided by RNIB to SNAP Cymru IPS and SNAP's involvement with the dyslexia-friendly schools project in Swansea.)

Recently the Legal Services Commission gathered together all the organisations in Wales who provide legal advice to families on educational matters, in order to begin the development of a co-ordinated network. Among that large group was a smaller but still substantial and diverse grouping of statutory, private and voluntary organisations that provide information, advice and support to families of children with SEN. There are arguments for the development of this network to ensure that Parent Partnership in all its forms is well coordinated in Wales.

A related initiative has been the setting up of the Wales SEN Partnership Forum following the SNAP Cymru consultative conference on the draft revised SEN Code of Practice in October 2000. The Forum's steering group, made up of voluntary and statutory organisations, has some parallels with the Special Education Consortium coordinated by the Council for Disabled Children and intends to monitor and advise on the implementation of the revised SEN Code of Practice.

The challenge of providing information, advice, support, self-advocacy, negotiation, mediation and everything that makes up the Parent Partnership package to all families of children with SEN (National Assembly for Wales 2002) will require an improved level of coordination, collaboration, innovation and investment. At present the story of SNAP Cymru's brand of Parent Partnership work is largely confined to Wales. We believe there is now a great deal to be said for sharing our experience further afield.

Acknowledgements

I would like to thank those people who have contributed to the development of SNAP Cymru over the years and to those who have assisted with this chapter.

Sources

If you would like a copy of the Partnership Charter or any further information about SNAP Cymru contact the author at:

SNAP Cymru
10 Coopers Yard
Curran Road
Cardiff
CF10 5NB
Email: roger.bishop@snapcymru.org
Website: www.snapcymru.org

References

Charities Evaluation Service (1998) *PQASSO – Practical Quality Assurance System for Small Organisations.* London: Charities Evaluation Service.
Department for Education and Employment (1998) *Meeting Special Educational Needs: A Programme of Action.* London: DfEE.

Department for Education and Employment and Department of Health (2000) *Guidance for the Education of Children and Young People in Public Care*. London: DfEE/DH.

Department for Education and Welsh Office (1994) *Code of Practice on the Identification and Assessment of Special Educational Needs*. Cardiff: Central Office of Information.

Department of Education and Science (1978) *Special Educational Needs: Report of the Committee of Enquiry into the Education of Handicapped Children and Young People*. (The Warnock Report). London: HMSO.

Gloucestershire LEA and SNAP Cymru (2000) *Service Level Agreement – Mediation/Conciliation Service*.

Hall, J. (1999) *Resolving Disputes between Parents and Schools and LEAs: Some Examples of Best Practice*. London: DfEE.

Jackson, S. (ed.) (2001) *Nobody Ever Told Us School Mattered – Raising the Educational Attainments of Children in Care*. London: British Agencies for Adoption and Fostering (BAAF).

Legal Services Commission (2000) *Community Legal Service: Quality Mark Standard*. London: Legal Services Commission.

Mukherjee, M., Beresford, B. and Sloper, P. (1999) *Unlocking Key Working: An Analysis and Evaluation of Key Worker Services for Families with Disabled Children*. Bristol: The Policy Press.

National Assembly for Wales (2002) *Special Educational Needs Code of Practice for Wales*. Cardiff: National Assembly for Wales.

Pembrokeshire Children's Centre (2000) *Inter-agency Service Co-ordination Proposals*. London: NCH Action for Children.

Roberts, G. (1989) *An Evaluation of SNAP Cymru*. Cardiff: SNAP Cymru.

SNAP Cymru (1998) *Partnership Charter*. Cardiff: SNAP Cymru.

Torfaen County Borough Education Department in conjunction with SNAP Cymru (1997) *Special Educational Needs: A Guide for Parents*. Torfaen LEA.

Urey, W. L. and Fisher, R. (1988) *Getting to Yes*. London: Arrow.

Vernon, J. (1999) *Parent Partnership and Special Educational Needs: Perspectives on Good Practice*. Research Report No. 162. London: National Children's Bureau /DfEE.

Welsh Office (1983) *The All Wales Mental Handicap Strategy*. Cardiff: Welsh Office.

Welsh Office (1999) *Shaping the Future for Special Education: An Action Programme for Wales*. Cardiff: National Assembly for Wales.

Wolfendale, S. (1992) *Empowering Parents and Teachers*. London: Cassell.

Wolfendale, S. and Cook, G. (1997) *Evaluation of Special Educational Needs Parent Partnership Schemes*. Research Report No. 34. London: DfEE.

Index